HOW TO TALK TO WOMEN

THE ULTIMATE GUIDE TO MASTERING
COMMUNICATION, STARTING CONVERSATION,
AND HOW TO FLIRT WITH CHARISMA,
CHARACTER, AND CHARM

NATE STRAUSS

PUBLISHING FORTE

INTRODUCTION

Women, women, and women – we cannot live with them and we cannot live without them. They are source of human race continuation and the caregivers of our family. Even though, women are just humans but majority of men find it difficult to understand the way they communicate.

Consequently, they experience clashes and conflicts. Moreover, there are men who fear having a conversation with women or simply shy away. Irrespective of your reason for lacking communication skills with women, the first step is to naturally understand how each gender communicates.

Once you learn the differing styles, it becomes easier to grasp signs and indicators that can LITERALLY steer the conversation in a different direction.

1. Body Language

Generally speaking, men tend to keep to themselves which is why their conversations seem to be practical and come across as serious. In terms of conversation, men just speak and listen that makes their conversation verbal most of the times. This includes intonation and vocabulary.

In contrast, women also utilize non-verbal cues when communicating. These are visual aids such as hand gestures, facial expressions etc. a common gesture exhibited by women is nodding their head. Another one incorporates hand movements to engage the audience and to display an open body language.

2. Facts or Feelings

The simplest way to get imperative information that is required is by getting to the nitty gritty right away. This is a strategy utilized by men generally. Majority of the times, men indulge in conversations that are based on facts.

Moreover, their conversations are mostly about finance, sports, work etc. Conversations might end abruptly and there is hardly ever a need for small talk. In addition, men do not ask unimportant questions.

On the other hand, women love to go deeper, be it conversations or relationships. They will normally try to figure out how the other person is feeling or what their intentions are while conversing with them.

It is especially true because women are seen to be highly empathetic and considerate. Female conversations revolve around complex situations and emotional states rather than fact based problems. A lengthy and elongated conversation is a typical trait of women.

3. Detail vs. Big picture

Men are always about the bigger picture whereas women tend to ponder over the little details. Women love going in depth and figuring out the root cause. Bridging this gap will help you to communicate effectively with women.

Try to see the picture from a woman's perspective rather than getting frustrated by the different style of communication. Exploring and looking at details is a natural instinct for women so do not disregard it. This is predominantly true for individuals who are looking for a love interest in the dating world. Understanding this will help you attract more women.

4. Compliments

When communicating, women tend to give out a higher number of compliments compared to men. Normally, men aim their compliments towards a prospective partner or a woman they are attracted to instead of a colleague. For women, giving compliments is a method of displaying respect and bonding.

Moreover, it is a sign that the person can be trusted and is not considered a threat. It also shows a woman's desire to develop connections and discover common grounds to converse. Complimenting a woman can be an excellent technique to initiate a conversation. Strike the right balance and you will find yourself talking to the woman of your dreams in no time.

5. Quality versus Quantity

Men do not like to elongate their conversation which is why you will find men in a rush to get to the point. Once they get their answers, the conversation comes to a halt. Workplaces tend to be super competitive.

Men in such surroundings will stay away from pointless dialogues and will not occupy themselves in niceties. On the contrary, women love having longer conversations, which can include queries about love or personal life. Questions might comprise of health, family, and even their plans for the upcoming holidays. Instead of involving themselves in competition, women tend to prefer cordial relationships and like to maintain a good bond.

Getting a grip on how women and men differ in the way they communicate can make your journey easier. This is fundamental to steer your efforts in improving conversational skills that might be lacking.

Your will find useful tips and methods that can be applied to talk to a woman in the best possible ways. All these tips and tricks will facilitate you get a date in no time.

WHY DO YOU FAIL TO ATTRACT THE WOMAN OF YOUR DREAMS?

As human we tend to have numerous encounters with different individuals in our life regularly. Some might leave a positive impact on us while others may not affect us one bit. Whatsoever the case be, every person is constantly drawing people in their life and it is completely fine if you are unable to gel in with all of them.

HOWEVER, when it comes to a romantic relationship or dating, majority of the times we believe that there is only one soul mate. All of us go from relationship to other in search of that perfect person. By having more than one unsuccessful relationship in life, you might feel as if there is something wrong with you. You will even start to question as to "why you always fail to attract the right person?"

ALTHOUGH THINGS MIGHT APPEAR to be smooth in the beginning but the spark finishes overtime. Eventually you end up blaming yourself for the incorrect choices that you made which make you feel miserable. In these moments, it is imperative to remember that relationships are not perfect and love is mysterious. But you must also be aware enough to not repeat the same cycle of attracting the wrong woman.

NOT BEING able to meet the right person does not have anything to do with your personal characteristics. It is not like you are not pretty enough or smart. But there are still some factors that pertain to you. If you are not meeting the right woman then it is probably because you are not in sync with what you are communicating.

LUCKILY, these variables are easy to alter and you will attract the woman of your dreams in no time.

1. Lack of positive Attitude

Similar to other areas of life, your attitude is a big denominator when it comes to your love life. This is because attitude impacts everything. It gives direction to your energy, thoughts, and the actions. Having positive energy and acting in the right manner can lead you to experience a vastly different outcome.

LIKEWISE, if you are consistently attracting the wrong woman then one of the main factors can be a lack of positive attitude. The first thing that you must understand is that you will always attract people who are your mirror image. So if you are constantly attracting the wrong woman then you should look at the energy and attitude that you are exuding.

· · ·

A LACK of positive attitude can mean a number of things. For starters, with a negative attitude, the level of confidence that you have will eventually shake. This implies that you will bring fear in the way you are expressing yourself which hampers the relationship before it starts.

FOR INSTANCE, if one of your ex cheated on you, then there is a chance that you will fear approaching other women. According to the principles of law of attraction, this attitude will eventually lead you to take actions that will make the women of your dreams cheat on you.

THE GIST: You must dig deeper and understand the factors that are leading you to fall for the wrong woman. With this recognition, you will be able to fix what is damaged, become more poised, and love yourself. As a result, this positive energy will draw in a more positive person.

2. Failure to Recognize Women Mindset

We all know that men and women have diverse mindsets and finding the right match is mostly made a challenge because of this. Majority of the men find it difficult to understand how a female brain works and this result in one of the biggest reasons why they tend to attract the wrong girl in their lives.

GIVEN that both the species have different mindset, it leads to a wide of expectations. Not being able to reach those expectations tend to failures in relationships. It is essential for a man to understand the mindset of the women they attract so that they can communicate and act accordingly.

. . .

FOR INSTANCE, women tend to be more sensitive and expect information more often. Maybe when the relationship is new, women act a "little cool" and pretend that they are not curious. If you expect that women will not want to know more in the future, then this mindset can backfire. You will start to bicker and argue about little things, which will destroy your relationship.

UNDERSTANDING the way women acts and thinks is also important for men because it will help them communicate well with the woman of their dreams. Women tend to be more dramatic in the way they communicate, which is new for men. When men fail to understand the female mindset, then they will act according to their own perceptions; causing further problems.

IF YOU ARE ATTRACTING a women who is constantly nagging; it will eventually make you negative and that will lead to a change in the attitude as well. Hence, you will be stuck in this cycle.

3. Understand Your Weak Points

No one is perfect. Each one of have strengths and weaknesses. Knowing your weaknesses is as significant as recognizing your strengths. These weaknesses that you mostly ignore can restrict you from truly chasing after your dreams and attaining a lot of amazing things in your life.

. . .

NOT ONLY WILL this facilitate you to strategize your life plan better; but it will also assist you in finding a woman who can complement these weaknesses.

YOUR WEAKNESSES ARE NOT something you should be ashamed of. Rather you must learn to identify, acknowledge and face them. This is one of the key aspects that will help you find the ideal romantic partner.

ONCE YOU REALIZE YOUR WEAKNESSES, you will be able to take the correct measures to improve those aspects of your life. For instance, if your past relationships have failed because of temperament issues; then you must get counseling or take up anger management courses. With this change, there will more stability in your mood and you will be able to attract someone with more positive attitude.

ANOTHER MAJOR WEAKNESS that a lot of men experience is trust issue. This is one of the worst things that can easily ruin a relationship. Without trust, there are two critical anchors that are missing: that are security and safety. If you are constantly experiencing jealousy, emotional infidelity, or lack of emotional support; it can attract the wrong woman into your life.

4. Try to Learn What You Want

This is an obvious factor of failing to attract the right woman. If you are not sure of the precise qualities you are searching for; then you will not know where to look. Having a clear vision for what you want in a partner is an important aspect that majority of people ignore, which also leads them to dating the wrong woman.

TRYING to figure out what you want might sound like a simple concept, however, it can be a bit more challenging as there are numerous variables involved. If you are not aware of the exact potential qualities in a partner, then you will be reacting to the powerful emotions of the moment and not selecting what your heart and head desires.

FOR STARTERS you need to identify the qualities you are looking in a woman of your dreams. This comes from understanding who you are and what your priorities in life are. Ask yourself what you are looking in a partner. But it is imperative to stay away from vague answers such as "someone nice." Vague answers will only confuse you. The definition of "nice and smart" might vary for people.

SO THE FIRST step is to figure out who you are and what is important for you. Are you shy or gregarious? Do you prefer the lazy life or love adventure? How much sex are you looking for? What kind of intimacy is perfect for you? These traits will facilitate you to select the kind of person and the place you can meet these individuals.

2

POWER OF TALK - HOW AND WHO GETS HEARD?

Communication and the power of talk is a blend of factors such as confidence, the words you use and the way you present yourself. As seen earlier, men and women differ in the way they communicate where female's communication system is intricate.

TYPICALLY, a female's method of communication is compared with an aircraft control panel that has an extensive range of knobs, buttons and levers. If you are looking to ignite an enticing conversation with women, then you will have to take note of certain characteristics that will catch a woman's attention.

THERE ARE certain principles or attributes that will make men more attractive to woman. Identifying and incorporating these attributes will increase your chances of being heard when you wish to converse with women.

Listening

Women are empathetic creatures who do like to be heard as well. If you are looking for an exciting conversation with a woman, it is imperative to display empathy and try to relate to their experiences and opinions. Make sure that when you talk, there are no distractions and you give them your undivided attention.

WHETHER YOU ARE APPROACHING a love interest or want to improve your communication with your partner, offering non-judgmental listening can do the trick. Simply hearing them out will take your relationship to the next level. This is especially true for married couples or people in a long term relationship.

WHEN YOU LISTEN TO THEM, women will appreciate it and will reciprocate. Attentive listening can also assist you to bring grand gestures to the table that can wow the girl of your dreams.

Intelligence

If you are planning to approach a woman at the bar, make sure that you have a valid reason for it. The biggest turn off for women is a dumb man. It is crucial to have a cute yet smart introduction rather than sticking to low-risk or basic intro-duction.

WHEN YOU WANT a woman to notice and to stay engaged in the conversation, you should have interesting topics and facts to add to the discussion. Girls love an intelligent man because they will never run out of experiences and stories to share about their adventures and other crazy discoveries. Creativity is the key to being heard and it will aid you in keeping the conversation going.

Humor

Statistics show that men who are funny have a greater chance of getting the girl because they know how to initiate a conversation. Moreover, they will find clever techniques to include witty remarks or make jokes that do not offend.

A FUNNY MAN can easily lighten up the environment and your mood, which is why women love to be around such men. You will win half the battle, if you can make your woman laugh without trying too hard. The trick is to ensure that you do not cross the line between a joke and being insensitive.

IF YOU CRACK a joke that crosses these limits, your chance of a second date is slim to none. Moreover, men who can laugh at themselves are seen to have a balanced personality which helps them be heard by women.

Inquisitiveness (About Her)

When you approach women, try to display that you have a genuine interest in which the woman truly is. Curiosity is the key to a thriving relationship as it will allow both (men and women) to enquire about each other.

. . .

WHEN YOU ARE keen to dig deeper and find out personal details, then you will be heard. Inquisitiveness does not mean that you bombard a woman with questions as soon as you meet them. It is a threatening sign and you will surely be rejected right away. If you wish to be heard, then try to be a man who truly wants to know your partner or the girl they are interested in. Do not judge, rather attempt to understand their reasons.

Exhibiting Respect

When talking to women, it is imperative to show them respect and to treat them equally. Envision this: what if you approach a woman and talk to them as if they are an inferior being.

Do you really think they would want to indulge in conversation with you? I don't think so. Men who exhibit respect and do not try to silence women tend to have a higher popularity in this modern world. If you want a woman to hear you out, acknowledge them as a resourceful person who contributes to the society.

MEN WHO SHOW respect and treat their woman as an equal will be heard more often as respect is a two way stream. Dominance in daily conversation or belittling women by ordering them around will only backfire as it can lead to instant dislike.

EVEN IF YOU have just met the girl, you need to value her opinion which is a form of displaying respect. Disregarding what they have to say or trying to prove them wrong will only put a bad impression and a woman will stop listening right away.

Emotional Presence

The focus on emotional intelligence (EQ) is rising because clash amongst relationship is caused by its absence. Having emotional intelligence will help you react and respond to situations in an appropriate manner so that no offense is taken.

MEN WHO HAVE HIGHER emotional intelligence will naturally have a higher presence emotionally. They will know when their partner requires space and when is a good time to talk about issues that truly matter. Male figures who have higher EQ will be able to offer support at the right time.

EVEN IF YOU meet a stranger to initiate a conversation, being emotionally present is essential. Otherwise, you will find yourself standing alone. This concept also incorporates being distraction free when talking to other people. Women are known to indulge in conversation with men who are emotionally present.

Sensitivity

If you are looking for an instant connection with a woman you have just met, then do not be afraid to show your sensitive side. Just like men have preconceived notions about women, similarly, women believe that men are unable to show sensitivity.

CATCH them off guard and be heard with a higher level of attention when you reveal your sensitive personality traits. It will also build a higher level of trust, making it easier to persuade them to go on a date with you. No man should come across as a chauvinistic prick because it will only make them lose interest.

Being expressive and articulate

Lastly, the best way to be heard is by talking freely. Majority of men shy away from expressing themselves or actually conversing when they are in front of other people. Being able to clearly talk with the girl you are interested in (crowds or no crowds) is a vital skill when you want to have a good conversation.

IT IS a skill that men must develop because smooth talkers are highly appreciated by women. Such men are heard more often compared to ones that shy away and act like someone else in front of people. If you are looking to attract a woman, hook them by the way you can hold conversations in public and how they openly communicate.

FREE COMMUNICATION WILL ALSO BUILD a meaningful and deeper connection. Even though, there are numerous other characteristics that will make women more attentive to what you have to say; but following these tips will drastically alter the way women see you. It will automatically improve your chances of getting the girl you like and will up your conversation game.

3

THE BEST WAYS TO APPROACH

With online dating apps and multiple indirect channels, people often wonder whether learning to approach a woman is relevant. In this modern and fast paced world, the concept might seem obsolete.

THERE ARE numerous online tools and sites that can facilitate you to connect with people and communicate with them without having to approach them. Even though, the latest technology is a huge help; however, majority of people still approach women face-to-face to develop a meaningful relationship.

BELIEVE IT OR NOT, this is an essential skill that is required to develop all sorts of relationships, be it friendly, professional, personal or romantic. Even if you are finding women through online dating sites, you will have to meet them in person. Not knowing how to approach a woman properly will decrease your chances of a second date.

. . .

LEARNING the best ways to approach a woman is essential if you intend to initiate a striking conversation. It is a key step if you are looking for a potential partner or plan on getting close to a woman. Luckily, the process of approaching a girl is simple and straightforward. Approach with confidence and you will see yourself attracting the woman of your dreams.

IF YOU ARE WONDERING how to approach women in a proper manner and make a long lasting impression, then check out these proven steps:

Do Not Exhibit Signs of Panic

Approaching a beautiful woman will surely put you in a state of panic. When you approach a stranger, you will be interjecting in their routine without prior warning. This is a major reason for feeling awkward.

THE STAKES BECOME HIGHER when you intend to approach a love interest because fear of rejection comes into play. Nevertheless, humans love to socialize when approached in a collected and calm way. Initially, figure out your reasons for getting nervous and the way you show signs of panic through your behavior.

FOR INSTANCE, if approaching a beautiful girl makes you nervous, then you can train your brain into believing that she is an old friend. This will make you feel calm enough to ensure a comfortable introduction. It will give you an internal confidence that can improve your chances of engaging with her.

. . .

RATHER THAN ASKING for her number right away, a better way to converse is to ask about something in the environment. For example, you can enquire about the drink she is having and whether or not they would suggest it.

OBSERVATION IS key here as it will allow you to extract topics from your surroundings. You must aim to make the interaction a mutual experience, which could be your commonalities, the bar experience you are getting etc. Try to avoid giving excessive compliments because it will only steer the conversation in an awkward place.

THE AIM IS to build a natural rapport to ensure a smooth journey. An aggressive approach will display signs of desperation which might make her uncomfortable.

Look For Signs That Show Interest

When it comes to approaching a woman, timing is EVERY-THING. Prior to worrying about how to approach or what to say, a crucial element is WHEN to approach a woman. Perfecting your move's time can be the difference between getting the girl of your dreams and losing her forever. So how can you tell when the time is right? It is simple. Notice the body language cues of the woman you are interested in. Observe whether the girl you want to talk to is staring at her phone, alone or with a group.

. . .

IF SHE IS CHILLING with her friends, chances are that she might not have noticed you and it might be difficult to determine this. However, there are a couple indicators that display signs that she is interested. For example, she might look in your direction more than once and even make eye contact.

IF THE WOMAN you are interested in has already sent a smile in your direction, then it shows that she is willing for you to approach her. Moreover, look for signs of positive mood and a relaxed body posture because it ensures that the woman is willing to socialize and indulge in a conversation. Knowing these body language cues will instill a level of confidence, which guarantees a better chance for a great conversation.

YOU MUST ALSO NOTICE signs of discomfort and definitely should not approach a woman. She might be having a bad day and will not welcome any stranger to hit on her. In addition, if a woman seems occupied with her friends or work, do not approach her because it will show your lack of observations and will lead to a bad impression. You must never stare as it will make her uncomfortable.

Approach from the Side

Women like to guard themselves because they fear being attacked. If you are looking to approach a woman, then make sure you walk from the side. If you approach a woman from the front or the back, chances are that the elicited response will not be desirable.

. . .

WHEN YOU WALK from the side, it allows a woman to be prepared as they will be able to see you walking towards them. Startling a woman will naturally make a bad impression and the conversation will take a direction that JUST won't be pleasant. Eventually, you should intend to strike the perfect balance where you do not approach the woman with them being completely unaware and also do not seem threatening.

Keeping an Open Body Language

When you approach a woman, it is not only about the inviting cues that they present. Rather, it is imperative for you to have an open body language so that both of you can be comfortable enough to have a conversation. Confidence is an attractive attribute but it should not be mixed with cockiness.

MOREOVER, when you talk to her make eye contact but avoid staring. Making eye contact every few second's aid in establishing a deeper connection, sense of closeness and a higher level of trust. Apart from that, an open body language includes keeping your hands in plain sight rather than holding them in a defensive posture.

Approach with Confidence

Approaching a woman will obviously make you nervous because you can't control the outcome. However, the actual tactic is simple: just pretend that you are confident. It is a striking characteristic and the woman you are trying to talk to will notice it. Being confidence (or pretending) will show that you are sure of yourself.

. . .

A GREAT CONFIDENCE building method is to assure yourself that you have few conversation starters on top of your head, and you did observe the signs rather than jumping into the impossible. Moreover, accepting the worst case scenario (she might not indulge in conversation) will also do wonders to boost your confidence.

MAJORITY OF MEN find approaching a woman to be the hardest part. If you can't do it on your own, bringing in a friend as your wingman can always help. Faking confidence will facilitate you to approach a woman and the rest will slide into place easily. Dressing up in proper attire and believing that you are a great person will augment your confidence level around girls.

Do Not Use an Aggressive Approach

Talking to a woman and making it work doesn't have to be a quick process. A desperate move that will definitely lead to a negative response is walking up to a woman and asking for her number. An aggressive approach such as this will only lead a bad impression and a straight NO.

YOU WILL RARELY FIND any man or woman feeling comfortable giving their number to a complete stranger. A better approach is to start small, talk a little, and get a drink. If they seem interested and you would like to meet them again, then leave your number instead of asking for their contact information.

WANT to help them know you better? Give them your social media handle rather than exchanging numbers. This is a two pronged technique. It will allow them to see your digital presence and find out a little more about you. In addition, it allows them to feel safe when contacting you.

Using Corny Pickup Lines

It's natural to be nervous when trying to talk to a woman (especially if you are shy), BUT try to find positive methods of dealing with this uneasiness. Avoid using cliché pick up line that will only get you an eye-roll. Women have a strong sense of catching this sort of crappy behavior.

So it is better that you plan your approach method by thinking of unique ways to present yourself. Moreover, these unoriginal pickup lines will create an uncomfortable and awkward aura that will lead to an opposite response. The best way to talk to a woman is by being yourself and work towards an organic connection rather than forcing yourself onto her.

When approaching a woman, having a genuine interest will help in developing a perfect connection. Ask questions that displays your true interest and exhibits that you care because it will show them that you really want to know them. Moreover, it will remove the notion that you are only physically attracted to them.

Be Calm About Rejection

Did you take note of the inviting cues? You were not aggressive? You were collected and cool rather than being pushy? So you did everything right but she still doesn't seem interested?

. . .

THAT'S OKAY! It happens. She might not be interested in you and you will just have to accept this fact rather than getting hyper. If she decides not to talk to you, simply smile and say something positive like "it was a worth a try. Have a nice evening." It will allow you to end the interaction on a positive note, which is a flattering for woman. Giving a compliment might make their day, which is an excellent alternative.

REMEMBER to keep realistic expectations which means having high involvement to the opportunity but low attachment to the outcome. In case, the plan doesn't work out you should be able to move on rather than feeling disappointed or heart broken. Moreover, you must remember that women have a right to choose and it has nothing to do with you.

DO NOT INTERNALIZE rejection or overthink why they did not like you. It is also imperative to never force the woman to change their mind or enquire why they are not willing to talk to you. It is super creepy and will make them feel threatened. Just accept and tell yourself that there are other women that will like you. Don't let one rejection put you down and generalize that all women will reject you. Practicing organic connections will surely bring you close to your soulmate.

4

PLAN BEFORE YOU WALK

Are you a smooth talker? Or do you struggle with making small talk with woman to get a conversation going? Even if you are confident, chances are that your tongue starts to stutter as soon you come across your crush or a beautiful woman.

INITIATING a conversation and keeping it interesting is a social skill that is not only crucial but is also useful. It can help you interact and act appropriately in a wide number of social settings such as impressing a client, chatting with a new colleague or acquaintance and even talking to a potential love interest. Moreover, mastering this skill can aid you in feeling confident that ultimately leads to a good talking experience.

WHEN IT COMES to approaching a woman and talking to them, many men shy away. If you are not good at communicating with women, then this segment of the book will offer some valuable lessons. Like all other areas of life, planning is key to a successful interaction. Fear of rejection or going blank can make you lose focus and put you off track. For this reason, you must have a plan in motion prior to walking towards the lady of your dreams.

PLANNING FOR A CONVERSATION with a woman should be thorough especially if you are anxious or a socially awkward individual. From approaching to having a well-thought out exit strategy; you should plan it all. It will save you from embarrassment and will help you be prepared for any hurdles and bumps that come your way.

Plan an Interesting Introduction

After approaching a woman, you obviously have to say something rather than just standing there to wait for magic to happen. Planning an introduction is crucial if you want to have longer conversation.

WHEN YOU DO NOT PLAN this, there is a high chance that you will get nervous right when you make eye-contact with the woman you want to converse with. You might go blank, which make you look the opposite of confident and smart.

KNOWING how to introduce yourself is essential because it sets the stage for further conversation. Planning for an interesting introduction is essential so that you are unforgettable if you are trying to attract a love interest. There are different techniques that can be applied when introducing yourself, including:

. . .

• QUESTION INTRODUCTION- "HEY, I'M MICK" is straightforward and low-risk, but is it memorable? We don't think so. Break the ice with creative question introduction. It could be cheesy. For example, if you are at a bar, you could say "Hey I'm Mick, what's your favorite drink?" Try to make your question appropriate to the surrounding you are in so that it seems relatable.

• OBSERVATIONAL AWARENESS INTRODUCTION- AS MENTIONED BEFORE, approaching a girl at the local coffee shop and saying, "ahh my name is Bill" won't really make the magic happen. An interesting way to introduce yourself to a woman is to pick out something from the environment and using it to lure them into conversation. For instance, you can say "Hiiii, I'm Bill and I have noticed that you and I enjoy a tall latte in the morning" It will surely catch their attention and can give you an opening for an exciting conversation.

IRRESPECTIVE OF WHATEVER method you decide to use, you should not be self-conscious because it is just a polite way to tell the other person who you are. Moreover, it does not indicate a romantic gesture. Developing a plan will keep you prepared for the worst and will protect you from making a fool out of yourself.

HOWEVER, some men make the mistake of over planning and repeat the entire conversation in their head over and over again. Moreover, exude confidence you approach a woman and ensure that you do not rush the procedure.

Have Some Conversation Starters in Mind

Imagine this: you find the courage to walk up to this girl you wanted to converse with, you introduce yourself and all of sudden the conversation just dies. This is the biggest mistake that men make when planning.

YOUR PLANNING PROCESS should incorporate a couple of top-notch conversation starters so that you can fill up any awkward silences. These conversation starters must, preferably, be spread over a broad range of topics so you can avail multiple chances to engross the woman you have reached out. Chalking out topics isn't the only smart move.

YOU MUST ALSO KNOW how to use them properly in the setting that you are in. For instance, if you are in a bar make sure that the conversation starts off by discussing the environment of the bar or their favorite drink. Moving forward, you can extend into several topics that interest you and the woman you are conversing with. You can ask them about their philosophy to live life, what eateries do they recommend or the subjects they enjoy. Take note of these answers because you can use them to further the discussion or take them out to places they really enjoy in the near future.

AT THE PLANNING STAGE, you can also add a questions to your list because they can add to the conversation directly. In addition, they allow you to dig deeper into the areas being discussed. When you ask questions, it shows that you are attentive to what she is saying and also displays your level of interest.

Compliments

As stated in the introduction, women love compliments and use it as a technique to bond and trust. For this reason, a segment of conversation starters should also include compliments. Questions can be ambiguous even when used in the introduction.

ADDING compliments to your conversation is essential for men who are approaching a woman they like. Complimenting will give them a clear message regarding your intentions. Although you can complement about anything, but it shouldn't be personal. When giving a compliment, do not overstep and make it about something noticeable. a woman

Make Sure You Have A Meet Up Plan In Motion

When you get the girl's number, never run off or exhibit signs of escaping from the conversation. Even though, getting their social media handle or number does call for celebration; but stick for a while longer.

AFTER YOU CAN TELL that they are interested in meeting again, you can build on this and suggest a meet up plan. You can also suggest chatting soon and send a video link that came up in the conversation. Just in case, think of a place in the planning stage so that you can bring it up while talking if all things go well. Don't act pushy or desperate about using the number.

Have An Exit Strategy

Your approach efforts and conversation can go in either of the two directions: very good or complete shutdown. Needless to say, you must have an exit plan for both scenarios. If things do not go well, you must already have a statement in mind to leave the place.

ENSURE that your one-liner keeps your integrity intact and respects the woman as well. You can say something like "Have a nice day or Maybe one day". On the other hand, if you did exchange social media handles or numbers and the conversation is just stalling; look for a good moment and excuse to end the conversation.

MAKE it look natural so that it does not look like you are escaping their presence. You can either make a place that you need to be or someone that you have to meet. Find a moment and tell the girl that you are running late and remind them that you will get in touch soon. After that, make a confident and swift exit (even if you don't want to).

5

HOW TO PRESENT YOURSELF?

First impressions count! Even though, it might seem like a cliché but a chance to rewind and erase your first impression is rare to come by. How you present yourself to a woman in the first meeting sets the stage for future interactions. Research suggests that the first seventeen seconds are crucial because a woman will observe your smile, your gait and how you present yourself overall.

A POWERFUL FIRST impression will lead to the "love at first sight" feeling, which is an excellent outcome if your aim is to find love. It is crucial to make a great first impression as it is a deciding factor of what the future will hold. After the initial impact with gestures, words, and how you look are considered to be secondary. There is not a lot your can do to change these impressions.

SO HOW CAN you present yourself for a lasting first impression?

Appearance and the Way You Are Dressed

Although you can't change your physical features (unless you opt for surgeries, which is not recommended), there are still certain appearances that people are attracted to. Looks are not everything but humans are mostly shallow creatures and tend to rely on the outer appearance; at least initially.

FOR INSTANCE, if you meet a woman and she is not dressed properly or has inappropriately applied makeup, chances are that you won't be attracted. Similarly, woman tends to notice a man's appearance even before they are being approached.

MOST OF US might not want to admit this, but looks and the way someone appears outwardly matters. Normally it is the first thing that attracts one person to another. Appearance is basically a person's physical features such as the way they dress, hygiene etc. The reason why appearance matters is because it is an indication of self-worth. How you dress up says a lot about who you are and how you feel about yourself.

STAYING FIT PHYSICALLY, being properly-groomed, and dressing suitably are signs that you respect and feel good about yourself. Moreover, it is also a representation of how you wish to present yourself. When you dress inappropriately, chances are that you dream girl might not prefer that even if you have amazing personality traits.

IT IS essential that you dress sharply but make sure that you feel comfortable wearing it. Do not wear something that is unique to the environment you will be in or only because a woman would want you to wear it.

WEARING what you like or are comfortable in will augment a positive attitude. Moreover, it will keep you in a better mood and will allow you to exude confidence. When you are planning on meeting a woman, you need to ensure that you smell good. However, you must not overdo it or smell like a perfume shop. Smelling good will blend well with your pheromones and will tingle her senses.

SIMILARLY, when you are dating online; your profile picture matters a lot. This just goes to prove how appearance plays a vital role in attractiveness. You may approach the woman of your dreams and she turns you down just because of the appearance. It is essential that you must ensure a proper appearance and dress according to the place and person you will be meeting.

First Few Words

As mentioned before, first impressions mean everything. You obviously don't want to be tongue-tied when you meet a girl. If smooth talking doesn't come naturally to you, it is important to prepare yourself beforehand.

THE FIRST FEW words you say to a woman when you approach them accounts for a major chunk of the impression that will be built and what the future holds in store for you. Keeping the introduction simple is a perfect idea. However, adding a little creativity can leave a lasting impression.

. . .

SURE YOU CAN SAY things like "Hey I'm Mike" but try to make a
memorable introduction. Ask a question that seems appropriate in the environment you are in when meeting a girl. For
instance if you meet the woman at a play, you can say "Hi
whose performance did you love"? Or you can say who do you
think you can play better? This is a great way to start a conversation given that a basic question like that would make them
respond and present you in an exciting way.

SHE WOULD WANT to know more about your views. If you can
walk away without telling your name, it will make her crave
you more. It is a perfect way to manipulate her without even
bringing the tactic in observation. Leave a little bit of the
mystery and suspense so that there is something you can talk to
her about later in the conversation.

LIKEWISE, presenting yourself well in online conversation is
also essential. You can start the conversation with a joke, or a
light question. A great way to begin the conversation is by
thanking them for accepting your request. If a woman does not
respond quickly, then you must not bombard them with question. It could be a sign that they are not interested or are busy.
Take the hint and react appropriately.

Treating Her Right

Imagine a person yelling at the valet or being rude to the wait
staff; it will essentially give off a negative impression. Similarly,
if you are on a date and you start to dominate the people
serving you; a woman will not be pleased.

. . .

WOMAN IN GENERAL are polite individuals who prefer kindness. If you are looking to impress a woman; then it is essential that you are on your best behavior. Tip properly, and thank the person serving you. Apart from that it is also imperative to be respectful of your date and even open the door to the car. A little chivalry will work wonders.

MOREOVER, treating the girl right and exhibiting good manners will help in image building and makes a great introduction. No woman would like a man who is self-obsessed and keeps talking about himself.

A GOOD MANNERISM doesn't only incorporate eating properly and opening doors for a woman, rather it also includes being courteous and polite. In addition, treating her right also means paying attention to the body language signs, listening carefully and not interrupting.

6

MAKING SMALL TALK

H ave you ever heard people talking about basic things such as the weather and then branching out further to topics that are actually interesting? This sort of communication tactic is known as making small talk. It is a style of communication that is informal and light, which can facilitate strangers to break the ice and reduce the level of anxiety experienced while initiating a conversation with an acquaintance.

EVEN THOUGH, some people might believe that small talk isn't that important and may consider it crucial; but it can help in establishing connections. This is especially true when you intend to create relationships on social events or in places you have to interact with strangers.

FOR PEOPLE who are looking to talk to women, knowing how to make appropriate small talk can make a huge difference.

However, not everyone has the skill to indulge in small talk in natural ways.

READ on to these easy to follow small talk steps/tips so that you can master the skill and gain valuable connections:

Keep Yourself Updated

In the world of social media, keeping up with the inflow of information might be a little difficult. But you do not want people discussing viral videos or news while you stand dumb founded.

FOR THIS REASON, you must dedicate a little time of the day to news and the latest events. It will help you be confident when conversing with people. You can follow some popular social media pages and remember to check them once a day.

Ask Open-Ended Questions

People love talking about themselves because it is easier and is far better than topics that you might be clueless about. While talking to a woman, asking open ended question can lead to unique and interesting responses.

MOREOVER, these questions allow you to move from shallow discussions to deeper emotional topics. All this will facilitate the other person to open up and talk about their interests, passions and hobbies.

Talk less, Listen more!

Everyone woman enjoys talking about themselves, which is why you should hone the skill to listen attentively. Being a great listener helps you in developing deeper connections. Bank interesting questions and then give the other person a chance to talk.

EVEN THOUGH, zoning out is a tempting behavior but you will not be able to dig deep. When you tune out, the other person will notice instantly and might end the conversation. In addition, when you listen carefully it can aid you in remembering details that can help you to ask relevant questions. Hence, it is imperative to practice active listening.

Avoid Distractions

The biggest distraction is our phone. Hearing a beep or a ringtone instantly makes us jump on our phones. When you are making small talk or generally conversing with people, it is imperative to be all-in the conversation.

IF YOU CONTINUOUSLY KEEP CHECKING YOUR phone, it will give the woman you are talking to an impression that there is something more important going on. It is a quick way to end the conversation and show that you are not genuinely interested. During awkward silences or when people become uncomfortable, the first thing that comes out is our phones.

NOTHING WILL INTERFERE with your efforts to make a conversation with the woman of your dreams then using a phone.

When you are scrolling through your phone, it will signal that you are busy or just not interested in mingling. It will decrease your chance of igniting a conversation.

Prepare For A Couple Of Safe Topics

If you aren't a natural at small talk, then a little preparation can take you far. When approaching a women, it is crucial to pocket some safer questions or comments to use when the conversation seems like a drag.

You could prepare with subjects such as the recent videos or memes, current events or talk about a famous celebrity posting things on social media. Moreover, you can also bank a couple of stories that can be told. For instance, you can talk about your latest hiking adventure or the road trip you took.

These stories will encourage the other person to share their personal experience that can keep the small talk on a roll. Interesting fact sharing also make as great conversation starters.

Don't Get Awkward in Silence

One of the biggest fear people tend to have about conversing with women is awkward silences. Stop panicking when there is a break in the conversation. These silent moments can allow the other person to process the details you mentioned. So rather than bombarding women with small talk questions, allow them to take their time to think through.

. . .

MOREOVER, silence can be a great way to transition from topics. It is imperative to notice indicators that the women you are talking to wants to escape the situation. Allow them to get away. If they still seem interested, throw in a statement that will reignite the conversation.

Ideal vs. Inappropriate Small Talk Topics

Walking up to a stranger (especially of the opposite sex) and starting a conversation can be extremely awkward. For this reason, majority of people bank small talk topics that can be utilized to break the tension in the environment.

THESE TOPICS CAN BE USED as a conversation starter and will give you the confidence to initiate a conversation with a woman. Overcoming your fear of making small talk is an excellent way to reduce the anxiety you experience.

TO FACILITATE YOU, we have gathered the top topics that are perfect for small talk, along with areas that must be avoided.

Ideal Topics for Small Talk

Weather – an ultimate small talk topic is the weather because everyone can talk about it. Even though it isn't the most exciting conversation starter but branching from it creatively can spark some interesting conversations. You can enquire about the person's plan contingent upon the weather.

FOR EXAMPLE, you can ask whether they are going to go on a hike, plan a BBQ or simple enjoy their meal outdoor on this beautiful sunny day. You can also take the discussion further by asking their favorite climate and it can also lead to the climate in their home town or their personality. If you are looking for an out of the box topic, then you can also bring up seasonal traditions or rituals in your city.

Food – One of the best small topics includes food when it is kept neutral. Everyone loves to eat, which is why no one would feel left out in this conversation. Moreover, it is a broad topic so the conversation can be kept interesting.

Talk about their favorite cuisine or the eateries they would recommend. Ask about whether they enjoy cooking or love take outs. These questions will help you understand their personality in a short time. You can ask questions such as "what do they enjoy cooking, do they prefer sweet or savory?

Work – another small talk topic that people resort to is by asking about your occupation. The conversation starter can lead to interesting observations and will help you stretch the topic to multiple arenas.

People will ask what you do, whether you are satisfied with the job you have, what motivated you to opt for this position? Try to take a step further and ask questions that are not typical. For instance you can ask about the stereotypes associated with this job and whether they are true?

· · ·

WHAT DO you dislike and like about your role in the organization or any advice they would give regarding their area of expertise. Remember that you must avoid uttering complaints because it can result in negative perceptions.

HOBBIES- HOW YOU UTILIZE your free time or how you intend to relax and enjoy little moments in life can be exhibited in the activities you indulge in. For this reason, people love enquiring about your hobbies and enjoy talking about theirs as well.

WHEN YOU ARE TALKING to a woman, hear them out and do not forget to ask a follow up question. It will show them that you are interested in their passion. As a result, they will get excited and would want to continue talking. This is an excellent topic that can lead to deeper connections.

THE OPPORTUNITY IS unlimited when you converse about hobbies. You can ask them if they will be willing to take up a new course or are already enrolled in any interesting programs. Moreover, similar hobbies can help you to figure out a common ground.

ENTERTAINMENT – every person has a different interpretation of entertainment. Some might love traveling for fun while other prefers to lie on their couch and binge watch movies. This is an amazing conversation starter and includes the discussion about popular eateries, music, movies and books.

· · ·

IF YOU ENJOY READING, then you can talk about your favorite book and whether they have read something worthwhile recently. Small talk intends to bridge the gap between two people and allows you to better understand one another. Traveling is another source of entertainment. Your previous vacation or the upcoming adventurous trip can contribute to your conversations. Discussing travel stories can be exciting and keeps the conversation light and positive.

Inappropriate Topics To Bring Up During Small Talk

Couple of topics is too complicated to include in an informal and casual conversation. These topics are best avoided because they can lead to strongly opinionated and chaotic discussions. Avoid these topics especially if you are approaching a woman you are interested in.

RELIGION AND POLITICS –Meeting someone new and bringing up these two topics can be risky. You will not be sure of the religion or political views that others in the environment hold.

THESE TOPICS generally lead to a heated discussion, which will defeat your purpose of impressing a girl. Likewise, religion will elicit some strong opinions from the crowd and is considered a sensitive topic.

OFFENSIVE JOKES - When approaching women or making a conversation with them, it is only natural to be nervous. Many people try to conceal their anxiety by cracking jokes that might come across as insensitive. These jokes should be saved for your best friend. When conversing with a woman, never make racist or sexist jokes because they are offensive.

MOREOVER, it will bring the conversation to an end abruptly. Some people might not feel that a joke could be offensive till they have already cracked it. So if you are planning to approach a woman for a magical conversation, make sure that your joke doesn't hurt or offend them, their gender, culture or race. It is best to avoid jokes if they are controversial.

PREVIOUS RELATIONSHIPS - RUNNING out of topics to talk can encourage you to talk about things that should be avoided when you meet a woman or while on your first date. One of the most common topic that men bring up is their previous relationships which is just the worst idea.

IF YOU ARE TRYING to develop a romantic connection, then talking about your ex can be a deal breaker. Consistently making comparisons and bringing up your past relationship can indicate that you are still hung up on your ex.

MOREOVER, it is a major turnoff and you will definitely not be going on a second date with this woman. Another reason that this is an inappropriate topic for small talk because it will show the girl how you would talk about them in the future if things don't work out.

ONE SIDED TOPICS – Ever had a conversation with something that was only about their highly technical job? Sounds boring?

Exactly. If you want to ignite an interesting conversation, then it is imperative to stay away from topics that the other person might be clueless about.

IT COULD COMPRISE of hobbies that are not practiced commonly or talking about a show that might not be very popular amongst the female crowd. This does not imply that you should avoid these topics completely, however, your initial discussions should revolve around general topics. Otherwise, the conversation will seem to be ONLY about you. It is best to notice signs that indicate boredom or confusion and quickly move from that topic.

Sex - If you are genuinely interested in a woman and want to talk to them in the long run, then bringing intimate statements or questions can be a problem. Small talk is used to break the ice or reduce the tension.

WHEN YOU TALK ABOUT INTIMACY, it could make the other person uncomfortable, which ruins the purpose of small talk. Meeting a woman for the first time and bringing up sex indicates that you are only interested in their body. It will bring your conversation to a halt sooner than you expect.

7

WORK ON NON-VERBAL CUES

Approaching and communicating with women is not only about using the right kind of words. Rather non-verbal cues such as your posture, gestures, facial expressions and tone of your voice all play a major role in making the interaction a success.

RECOGNIZING the importance of nonverbal cues and communication can create a huge difference. Exhibiting proper body language when talking to women can augment the level of clarity and trust.

YOUR BODY LANGUAGE can easily give away your intentions. If the woman you are trying to have a conversation with thinks that you are distracted, annoyed or bored; they will instantly escape or end the conversation.

. . .

MAJORITY OF THE TIMES, people are unaware of the body language cues they are presenting and how it impacts their interactions. So if you want to talk to a woman, you must be aware of the non-verbal cues you are presenting.

So What Exactly Is Non-Verbal Communication?

Nonverbal communication comprises of a variety of nonverbal cues that express different emotional states and balance out the verbal messages.

THIS TYPE of communication uses number of body parts, which may be used in a way consciously or appear involuntarily. For example, the head nod or handshake is non-verbal communicators that are voluntary. Other behaviors such as a shiver in the tone indicate nervousness or fright which is revealed on a subconscious level.

IT IS imperative to understand diverse kinds of communication skills because it allows you to control what you plan on expressing. Moreover, it will also facilitate you to decipher other people's emotional state. If you are looking to communicate effectively, then read on to find a couple of ways to comprehend nonverbal cues:

Demonstrating Interest

Nonverbal communication is an excellent method of showing engagement and alertness. People around you can observe different signs that show your genuine interest. When you alter your posture and make an appropriate eye contact, it will display that you are actually interested in what the other person has to say.

To Establish Connection

Another reason why non-verbal communication is amazing is because it leads to a higher level of trust and establishes a deeper connection. These communication gestures are sometimes universal. Such gestures incorporate hug or handshakes which are often seen as signs of greeting someone in almost all cultures.

For Conveying A Meaning

You will find a number of words that have several meaning. The words remain the same but your tone of voice can change its meaning. It can typically lead to misinterpretation, which can be avoided by learning how to match the non-verbal cues with your words.

To Display Authenticity

When it comes to establishing genuine feelings with the person you are communicating with, nonverbal communication can play a vital role. Making eye contact, having proper posture and having a genuine smile will show people that you are tapping into your true feelings.

Body Language Signs That Make Men Attractive

Have you ever heard women talking about what they find attractive in men? Notice that the features always come down to body language or non-verbal cues. You will hear women discussing how a particular man was walking or was dressed that made him sexy.

EVEN THE TINIEST thing such as the way a man's shirt is buttoned can be a major turn on. Women generally observe the little gestures that are exhibited by men naturally (which is part of why it makes them attractive).

SO IF YOU are looking to initiate a conversation with a woman, it is imperative to learn how to use these body language cues so that any woman is attracted instantly. Having proper body language is essential because a woman reads it before you even approach them or try to have a conversation.

IT LETS them access you and come to a partial decision before you even begin the conversation. Adjust your body language to have a higher level of attraction if you want to converse with a woman you recently me. These body language signs incorporate:

HAVING A Strong Body Posture

CONFIDENCE IS an attractive quality and ensures clarity and a higher chance of igniting an interesting, memorable and impactful conversation. This is especially true for women because they love a strong and confident man. Inherently, women see men as their shield which can be seen from the way they carry themselves.

.   .   .

STANDING with a hunch or slouching shows that a man will not be able to protect you against danger. For this reason, you must always a straight posture. If you want to exude confidence, then stand tall and it will make you attractive to a woman.

DO THE "SOFT EYES" Look

CONTRARY TO THE popular belief that men are only attractive when they display dominance, there are couple of tactics that can be used to lure women without being assertive. For instance, one of women's favorite body language is when a man looks at them with soft eyes.

RESEARCH SUGGESTS that soft gaze makes a woman's heart melt and make them feel beautiful. Moreover, the soft gaze indicates a sign of love that keeps women on the edge.

LET your Shoulders Talk

HAVE you ever seen a person with slumped shoulders? Do they look bored, nervous, scared and uninterested in the events around them? When a man has slumped shoulders, a women will not be attracted to them or want to have a conversation.

IF YOU ARE LOOKING to be irresistible, you must approach a woman with pushed back shoulders. It will make you look confident and interested in the conversation. Moreover, if you want to appear sensitive and sweet, raise the shoulders a few times.

Face Towards The Woman

THIS IS COMMON SENSE. If you are looking away from the person who are having a conversation with, it depicts your disinterest. When conversing with a woman, having genuine interest is essential because it increases your chances of a long term relationship.

A SURE SHOT way to show interest is by facing towards her at all times. This doesn't imply that you start staring at her but you should not be distracted. Turn in her direction so that the woman can feel your presence.

Making Eye Contact

SIMILAR TO LOOKING towards the woman, having good eye contact can also increase your chances of having a great conversation. This does not imply that you should straight out stare at the woman (because that is just creepy), rather you must make occasional eye contact. Eyes speak to the mind directly and you can use it to attract her.

DECENT and appropriately timed eye contact will facilitate you to establish a good rapport even before you begin the conversation. Maintaining eye contact with the woman you are talking to allows them to know that they have your undivided attention.

As a result, you will appear to be trustworthy compared to men who are unable to hold their gaze. Studies show that a prolonged eye contact can help your body release feel good hormones, which leads to attraction and feelings of love.

Listening Attentively

Who doesn't love being heard? During a conversation with a woman, listening carefully can be a real lifesaver. It will augment your chance of getting a second date and will make you irresistible.

If you are interested in this woman, listen to them attentively even if they are talking about mundane topics. This is one of the most imperative cues that make a person attractive. Remembering details that were talked about early on can surprise and excite a woman, making them feel special.

Do not back off

Approaching a woman comes with some nerve-wrecking thoughts, which can make you do crazy things. If a woman leans towards you, some men will back away. This is a major mistake because a woman will interpret it as if you are closed off or just not interested in the conversation.

. . .

IN SUCH MOMENTS, you can either stand your ground or lean forward to show you interest. Backing off will make the woman feel rejected and she might start looking for ways to escape the conversation.

HAVE a natural smile

IT IS NOT important that a topic that might interest a woman will particularly be something you enjoy talking about. In these moments, a fake smile is a polite gesture if you want to show that you are having fun.

HOWEVER, if you are romantically interested in a woman; try to avoid this. A woman can instantly catch when you are faking it because they will be noticing your facial expressions. A fake smile can be easily caught through the eyes. There is a major difference in eyes when it comes to genuine or fake smiles.

EYEBROWS GIVE AWAY A LOT!

ONE OF THE most neglected body language cue is the eyebrows. It plays a major role in the way a woman will view you. For instance, when the eyebrows are raised too high in a conversation, it comes across as rude.

. . .

WHEN CONVERSING WITH A WOMAN, if the eyebrows aren't raised at all, it depicts that you are uninterested in the conversation. Knowing how to talk through your eyebrows will increase your chances of a smooth conversation. Raising them just right will tell the woman that you are interested in them.

LIPS GIVEAWAY **sexual vibes**

EVEN IF YOU are meeting a woman for the first time, you may experience unquestionable sexual tension. If you are looking to establish that, make it a point to touch your lips a couple of times while having a conversation with her. Women are drawn to men who subtly touch their lips without even being aware of it.

WHEN YOU BEGIN TO OBSERVE, reading body language isn't that tough. These body language signs are being noticed at a subconscious level. In these moments, men or women determine whether the person exhibiting these signs is worth interacting with. After you master the art of subtly including these gestures, you will be able to attract the woman you have been yearning to talk to.

How To Improve Non-Verbal Communication?

Ever wondered the percentage of our non-verbal communication? Believe it or not, it makes up to 50-70% of our communication.

. . .

THIS KIND of communication is difficult to hone or polish because it appears naturally and happens at an unconscious level. Moreover, it is a major part of our personality. There are numerous ways of improving non-verbal communication including:

AWARENESS

NATURALLY, your first step to improving any skill requires you to be aware of the actions and behaviors exhibited. Once you have the awareness of what communication cues need to change, you will be able to streamline the process of change.

YOU WILL START to put in effort in that direction. At the beginning, these alterations may seem unusual. The trick is to fake it before these become a natural part of your non-verbal communication.

WORK ON BODY Language

WHEN IT COMES to communicating with women or in your workplace, your posture matters to a great extent. Certain body language gestures are known to show defensiveness or demonstrate that you are not comfortable with a topic or person. These incorporate turning away from others, having a rigid posture, fidgeting, cross your arms and legs or even slouching.

. . .

PEOPLE YOU ARE CONVERSING with might see these as offensive or off-putting gestures. For this reason, you must be cautious of your posture and standing position. It is imperative to keep a distance when sitting or standing with others when communicating.

IN ADDITION, you can work on having a relaxed posture or facing the person you are talking to. One way of improving these skills is by filming yourself and analyzing your body language.

Do Not Invade Personal Space

PEOPLE from different cultures might have different preferences or norms when it comes to touching and proximity. However, every person and culture has rules about respecting personal space.

IF YOU WANT to improve your communication skills, then working on this factor is imperative. If you stand too close to a person, you might end up making them feel uncomfortable and that might hamper the quality of conversation.

Relax Facial Muscles

EYES and your facial expressions tend to communicate a lot. A frown or a miserable expression will make the other person uncomfortable. They might stop listening to what you are saying and start focusing on the facial communication. For this reason, you should learn to relax your facial muscles and smile often.

To COMMUNICATE BETTER, it is essential to make eye contact because it demonstrates respect and honesty. When conversing with a woman or even a man, a prolonged eye contact can make the other person uncomfortable.

VOICE TONE, Speed, And Pitch

A MONOTONOUS TONE can be annoying and dull, making it difficult for others to concentrate on what you are saying. To improve communication skills, try to be a little lively as it shows a genuine interest.

NERVOUSNESS CAN MAKE YOU BREATHLESS, and your voice might get higher or softer. Projection of voice plays a significant role so you must practice that for better communication. One way to develop the right pitch is by doing breathing exercises. When people are nervous, they start to speak really fast which can make it difficult for others to understand. Talk clearly and slowly so that the listener can grasp what you have to say.

APPEARANCE

EVEN THOUGH, it might not make sense but your appearance is a type of non-verbal communication. When approaching a woman, a neatly dressed and well-groomed man has a higher chance of having a successful conversation.

A PROPER ATTIRE for the occasion displays that you are interested in the outcomes and respect another person's time.

TO GET a complete grip on non-verbal cues and communication, you must learn to read other's body language.

IT ALLOWS you to interpret whether a topic is boring the woman you are having a conversation with or if they are confused by the technical terms you keep using. In such situations, it is imperative to move on from the topic naturally and re-engage the person.

8

CREATE A DEEPER CONNECTION

Building a deeper connection is a desire that every human craves. We are social animals and we love a company that we can trust and share with. Although work relationships are different, but personal relationships require you to put in time and work.

IT IS these relationships that will help us mature, become successful and facilitate us to enjoy and share moments that matter. Deepen your relationships with family, friends, your partner, peers, and even the woman of your dreams.

IF YOU ARE LOOKING to build a stronger and deep connection with a woman or anyone, follow the tricks mentioned below:

Smile

Building a connection with people might not be easy but simple tactics such as smiling can help you to connect within seconds.

WHETHER YOU PASS a cheerful smile to stranger or offer tender and loving smile to a loved one, it will only deepen the level of association. Smiling is contagious and a heartfelt smile can lighten the mood and even makes someone's day. Your smile can leave a positive impact on someone and that can build connections.

Dig Deeper

When it comes to deepening relationships with others, it becomes essential to find out more about yourself and go through a phase of personal development. As you get to know more about yourself, it creates awareness of your priorities and who you would want to connect with. Inevitably, it facilitates you to identify what role each individual plays in your life and how important they are.

IT ALSO REQUIRES UNDERSTAND your emotions and how you feel about others. You might see changes in behavior patterns and belief systems. After identifying these aspects, you will be able to create a deeper connection with the woman of your dreams. When your awareness level increase, you will also see other people's perspective, which will allow you to deepen the relationship.

Be Attentive

How would you feel if you are talking and the other person is just looking around? Neglected, humiliated or suddenly uninterested in the conversation? Similarly, when you talk to a woman it is imperative to notice and observe the little details.

THIS WAY you will be able to learn a lot about the woman and use the information to show meaningful gestures. If you keep scanning the room or look at your phone every few minutes, then it will come across as rude and will display that you are not interested.

WHEN YOU SHOW signs that you do not care, you will NEVER be able to have a stronger connection that you are yearning for. Make sure that you make eye contact, ask interesting questions and compliment the woman. Moreover, you must concentrate on getting to know the person especially when you are short on time.

Display a Caring Attitude

One thing that will never go out of style is kindness and being empathetic. These characteristics play a vital role in creating a deep and strong connection with the woman of your dreams and are absolutely free of cost. Show how grateful you are that they gave you their time and how much you enjoyed the conversation with them.

IT LAYS the foundation of deeper connections as it demonstrate that you are human. In addition, it exhibits that you observe and appreciate little things in life. When you have a positive personality and display courtesy to people around you, it facilitates in building bonds that can last a lifetime. This is an imperative factor if you are searching for real friendships and long lasting relationships.

Be Open to Sharing

Every individual has their own goals, belief and thoughts. One of the best ways to deepen your relationship with a woman or with anyone else, is by being willing to share those ideas and what you are passionate about. Sharing a bit about yourself such as what you believe in is essential to create curiosity.

IT WILL ALSO MAKE them engage with you more often. If you have lived an interesting life, talk about that because it will make you memorable. People will associate these experiences with you and it will help them remember you.

IT OBVIOUSLY DOES NOT MEAN that you TALK all the time and do not give the other person a chance. You should make sure that your conversations are not lectures because it will just bore the other person. When you talk about something that entices you, the emotions that flow with it will be genuine and will aid in developing stronger connections. Moreover, it can also initiate friendly debates that can keep the conversation going.

Establish Likes and Dislikes

Everyone has skeletons in the closet. When conversing with people, it is imperative to understand the no-go topics so that awkwardness does not emerge. For this, you will need to dip deeper and find out what the other person likes and dislikes.

· · ·

ONCE YOU ESTABLISH that it will becomes easier to have deeper conversations. Moreover, profound connections will also help to understand the boundaries. Crossing these limits can compromise the relationship, be it in the family or working ties. You can do this by enquiring what the person holds important and what qualities will be a deal breaker.

Be Authentic

Finding authentic people is difficult and rare. If you are looking to develop a profound connection with the woman you love, then make sure you present yourself as authentically as possible. The major reason for failure in relationship is when one person pretends to be someone who they are not.

GENUINENESS IS tough to practice because you will have to see through and face your vulnerabilities. Being authentic means that you will have to share your personal stuff with the other person and be a safety net for them to share their insecurities. It is a sure shot way to connect with others and deepen the relationship.

IF EVERYTHING IS WORKING out great for you, try and help others by giving them motivation and inspiration rather than shoving your victories in their face.

Live in the moment

With such fast paced lifestyles, people no longer ask others about how they are or who they are. Stop for a moment and ask your loved ones about their hobbies, families, passion, goals in life and their ultimate vision about life.

. . .

USE your active listening skills when they respond. Ensure that your presence is great and you relate with them through non-verbal cues. When conversing with a woman, be present in the moment rather than thinking about your appointments or business meetings. Avoid using your phone or indulging in mindless distractions. The way you engage with others in person will define the vibe of the relationship. Being present and offering your undivided attention to the person will automatically deepen the connection.

Stand out of the crowd

Sometimes, creating a deeper connection requires you to show off your unique qualities or sense of style. Maybe you love wearing eccentric clothes, or only wear your signature color. Your clothes and your sense of style can be a great way to start a conversation.

WHEN YOU STAND out of the crowd, people will see you and will want to find out more. It will spark an interesting conversation but you might also risk being a joke of the town. Some people might even see your uniqueness as offensive. Connections that are real and you will be able to associate with these people on a deeper level.

DEEPER AND PROFOUND connections are essential for every human because it gives us a sense of fulfillment. Apply these strategies and make friends that matter. Such relationships go a long way and will keep you grounded.

9

ANXIETY AND FEAR

D o you ever roll your eyes as soon as you hear someone say, "Making conversation at a date is exciting and fun!" it is true though, communicating with new people and dating is supposed to be fun. It gives you an opportunity to dress up, hang out with a new person, eat something delicious and watch movies. Most people find that stuff entertaining.

YET, there is definitely more to it than excitement. There is the messaging. The vulnerability. The questioning. The awkwardness. And all the feeeeeeeelings. Given all these factors, having a conversation with a woman can be pretty stressful.

STRESS DOES NOT ALWAYS HAVE to be a bad thing but figuring out a way to adapt or cope with the stress in a way that is healthy is significant. Besides stress is inevitable; so if you try to avoid it chances are that you will only experience a higher level of stress. As is commonly said, what you resist persists.

. . .

THAT DOES NOT MAKE it any easier to manage the unpredictable patterns dating and conversing with a woman has. Mostly, women would give anything to know if their crush is really searching for something serious. In addition, women have had incalculable discussions trying to help their friends decode the mixed signals that are passed on. Or it could be you who has been sending mixed signals.

ALL THE CONFUSION and stress makes it enticing to straight up ask, "Hey! Do you like me? And, would you like to be with me?" This is easier said but only a very few people will have to the guts to ask a woman this straight question. It is scary to put yourself out there and possibly get hurt. Nobody likes getting hurt or looking silly.

IF YOU ARE CONSTANTLY FEELING anxious or being fearful of conversing with a woman, then this segment of the book will help you. When you start to feel anxious, keep the following factors in mind as it will aid in alleviating your fear.

Odds Are, There Is Nothing Wrong With You-

If one person rejects you, it does not mean that there is something wrong with you neither should you assume that you will be alone all your life. Rather identify what went wrong. Maybe the other person was not your type.

MAYBE YOU DID NOT DRESS NICELY or maybe the timings just wasn't right. There could be a number of reasons for a failed conversation in the first meeting but what you need to remember is that THERE IS NOTHING WRONG WITH YOU. Repeat this whenever you feel stressed about communicating with women.

Staying Anxious And Fearful Will Get You Nowhere

You need to realize that getting all wound up about how the conversation is going to go or what will happen next, serves no purpose at all. All it does is mess up the overall experience and takes a huge toll on your sense of self and self-esteem.

CARING TOO MUCH ONLY LEADS you to want a certain outcome, investing all your mental energy to make sure things happen the way you want them to. When it does not happen, it causes disappointment. Just relax and go with the flow.

The Anxiety You Are Encountering Right Now Should Be Balanced By A Good Amount Of Fun

Experiencing stress especially when communicating with a beautiful woman is normal but stress without a little fun is torturous. Avoid doing that and look for ways to make your dating experience exciting and fun.

ONCE YOU HAVE a plan in mind and are confident about it, chances are you will overcome the stress.

Been Married Before? Does Not Mean The Same Rules Apply

Many people are re-entering the dating game for various reasons such as divorce, death of the spouse, separation etc. Just because you were married once does not mean you are a relationship expert.

PEOPLE BELIEVE that all the relationships are similar, although that is not true. So if your previous marriage did not end on a good note, does not mean that the history will repeat itself. Rationalize the negative thoughts by understanding that every woman is not the same and your next experience will be a great one. Rather than freaking out, find out new ways to deal with conversation anxiety.

Keep Fighting Fear & Grow Confidence

Initiating a conversation with a woman is something you will have to go through if you want to attract your love interest. If you keep practicing making conversation without backing down, you will definitely build courage and conversing with women will become a piece of cake.

EACH TIME that you walk up to a gorgeous woman, it will make you confident. Approaching a woman will reduce your level of fear and it will make you excited. Every time you face your fear and approach a lovely lady, you slowly but surely grow more confident. Fear starts to lose its grip. Your strongest feeling becomes excitement. You become naturally courageous.

. . .

CONVERSATION ANXIETY STEMS from imagining the worst scenarios that might transpire. When you keep practicing with women, it will show you that the negative scenarios are not part of the reality. In case a woman displays signs that she is not interested or straight out rejects you, then so what? Just move on! You will come across plenty of other women. However, if you don't approach a woman because of your fears, there is no telling whether you will be rejected or get a date.

Your Heart Is Brave

So what if the first date was not too much of a success. What does it matter if you are rejected? Remember you have a brave heart that is strong enough to take such challenges. Although it is an exaggeration that loves is a battlefield but it does require you to be brave to get out there and ask someone out. Do not fear- just have some fun.

ANXIETY AND FEAR of conversation with women will hinder your chances of getting a date. When walking up to a woman, make sure you do it with confidence. A strong posture will aid you to look and feel more confident in your ability to impress the woman. Once you are able to overcome this fear, you will realize that things aren't as bad as you imagined.

10

COPING UP WITH FEAR OF CONVERSATION/REJECTION

I t is normal to be stressed about communicating with potential dating partners. Everybody gets worried about making a great or at least a good first impression. When you see a beautiful woman, it is common to experience some sort of anxiety.

LIKEWISE, it is normal to reflect upon whether the person you are attracted to, likes you enough to keep the conversation going or will you be rejected.

AT TIMES ANXIETY, shyness, and the fear of rejection can hold you down. It can keep a man from attaining the love life they desire. BUT these feelings do not have to be bottled up anymore as you can overcome the fear of approaching a woman, having a meaningful conversation and avoiding the risk of getting rejected. All it takes is a little bit of effort and practice on your part, and it will help you control this fear.

· · ·

OVERCOMING the stress of having a proper conversation is not as difficult as perceived. First things first, you need to build confidence. More than feeling confident, you need to LOOK confident. Yes! You read that right.

WHAT MANY OF you do not know is that looking confident automatically elicits feeling of confidence within. Each one of us is very self-conscious as to what we say in a social gathering so we can fit in better. Confidence is the ability to act naturally.

WE PICK up confidence by overcoming obstacles, by demonstrating to ourselves that what we have been told about our (absence of) capacities is not as true as it seems. Do not let go of the opportunities only because you feel that there is a lack of capability. The best way to over the fear of having a conversation is by building confidence.

WHILE CONVERSING WITH A WOMAN, do not put up a front that does not imitate your true personality. Some people do this because they feel like they are not good enough on their own. When you gather confidence, it improves your self-esteem.

BEING honest and being yourself only reduces the stress because if you plan a facade it will only worsen the experience. If you lie throughout the date to present yourself as more appealing and interesting it will only stress you out more. Therefore, be true to yourself.

. . .

MEDITATE before you go out and meet for the first time. Meditating relaxes you. This does not necessarily have to mean that you need to get a yoga mat and practice a few yoga techniques. You can listen to music, watch a movie, etc.

IT COULD BE anything that relaxes you. You can also tell your friend to give you a pep talk before you go out on your first date. Your friends can always help you review your best qualities and bolster your confidence. Before leaving do a last minute mirror check because looking good is part of a great dating experience.

FOCUS on the positive outcomes when it comes to conversing with a woman. Do not read negative stories of how a conversation can go wrong on the internet. This only makes you believe that something like that would happen to you as well. Be open minded to new experiences and ideas and just enjoy the moments of the present. Pay attention to the little positive things like laughs, jokes, and interesting opinions.

AN EXCELLENT METHOD of reducing this fear is by directing your attention on the potential partner rather than yourself. Listen to what they have to say, focus on their words, look at their body language, eye contact and smiles. Communicate with them and stay "outside" of yourself, overlook your internal responses, and concentrate on making the evening pleasant. Do not get stuck on your concerns, opinions or thoughts instead remember what they liked, felt or thought about you.

. . .

LASTLY, do not obsess about searching your perfect soul mate because let's admit it- we are not in a fairy tale. Perfection is a theoretical concept. Nobody is perfect and if you look for perfection, chances are you will end up alone. Learn to deal with imperfections otherwise, the increasing pressure will eventually catch up to you.

Go on fun dates and have deep conversations. Do not make your dates into stuffy interviews. Show up looking amazing, and have a great time. If it does not go well, you do not have to schedule a second date. It is as simple as that. This attitude will make it easier for you to be present fully and live in the moment. This way even if you were not perfect for each other, you would still have a good time, which could be the beginning of a new friendship.

Developing Confidence And Self-Esteem

Self-esteem is the feeling individuals have when they think about themselves. It imitates people's view of personal abilities and traits. A person with high self-esteem tends to appreciate themselves and people around him. They mostly find fulfillment and meaning in their lives and enjoy the joy in ordinary things. Usually a person with high self-esteem would believe in solving problems rather than focusing on the problem.

WHEREAS A PERSON with low self-esteem would focus on pleasing people, making them feel depressed and anxious. They tend to doubt themselves and regularly experience emotions of sadness and worthlessness. They question their abilities which leads to negative thoughts. Such an individual will naturally find it difficult to approach a woman and initiate a conversation.

MAJORITY of the individuals tend to base their self-esteem on outside factors, like their financial status, their weight, and whether other people will appreciate them or not. When these external variables alter, it broadly impacts the self-esteem. This is mostly seen in relationship when people risk feeling vulnerable and their self-esteem is based on someone else's love.

SO HOW CAN you develop a high self-esteem to ensure a great conversation and a long term relationship with women?

IF YOU WANT to develop your self-esteem and augment levels of confidence and self-awareness, then you must take note of your abilities and strengths. Being satisfied with who you are plays a vital role in building a higher esteem. This "inner peace or being at peace" does not imply that you are uninformed of your weaknesses; it just describes that you acknowledge who you are and sincerely like what you have become.

TAKE the following measures to develop a self-esteem and build confidence:

Stop Comparing Yourself With Others.

Most of the time, people who have a low self-esteem tend to make comparison with people who have accomplished a lot. When comparison comes, the outcome is completely disregarded. If you start comparing, chances are you will feel a lot worse and it endorses a lower encouragement.

THE PROBLEM IS that comparison is only made on certain elements rather than the overall picture. Rather than evaluating with others, concentrate on what makes you content and establish your own standards to live by. For instance, a richer guy might get the girl of your dreams. However, it should not bring you down because the girl might have seen other elements before choosing.

Body Language

When building self-esteem, be aware of the body language you are exhibiting. People with high self-esteem do not have an arched back or hanging shoulders. Rather they walk with pride and confidently. It is empirically proven that the way you walk impacts the way you feel. So in order to build a higher self-esteem you must walk face up, shoulders pushed back and with a straight back.

ALTHOUGH IT MAY FEEL odd in the beginning but you will feel confident soon. Improve the way you communicate by making eye contact, and expressing coherently. In addition, a great posture can have a constructive outcome in the way you feel about yourself. When you stand up straight and hold your shoulders back; your brain will figure out how to take after these positive body prompts, making you feel confident.

Don't Put Yourself Down

When you talk about yourself negatively, it will give you an idea that you are not good enough. This will lead you to perform worse than you actually are and you will be stuck in a vicious cycle.

TRY to break this cycle and you will be able to augment the self-esteem. In order to do so, you can write the positive you acquire. You can begin by writing 5 things and read them to yourself every day. Be conscious of the fact that you are putting yourself down and stop it immediately.

Evaluate Certain Friendships

It is possibly the most difficult task, however, it is imperative. Certain friendships have an ulterior motive where they either feel important in your presence or compare with you to feel better. If some of your friends are constantly demotivating you, gossiping, are not sincere, never compliment, or only concentrate on what you do not have; then it's time to let them go.

STOP ALLOWING these people to use you and avoid meeting them. To increase your self-esteem, you must surround yourself with individuals who are positive and offer constructive criticism.

Talk To Yourself

Self-talk is a significant means of enhancing your self-esteem. By communicating with yourself, on a conscious level you persuade yourself that you can attain anything. The idea behind self-talk is the same as utilizing your body language to influence yourself that you are self-reliant. Ultimately, the performance is impacted positively. If you talk yourself into talking to a woman, it will help you have a smooth conversation with them.

Accept Compliments

This might be a difficult task for individuals with low self-esteem. However, it is crucial to building a higher esteem. For starters, do not shy away from compliments that are received by friend, relatives, or even acquaintances. Just politely say Thank you.

IF SOMEONE COMPLIMENTS YOUR WORK, do not tell them the hard work that went in it, because this will take away the power of the compliment. Try and write why you are having difficulty in accepting compliments.

Is it because you have a negative viewpoint towards yourself? If so, then be open to accepting new ideas. Similarly if a woman is trying to compliment your dress or your hair, do not get stuck in a spiral of negative thoughts. Accept that she might be flirting with you.

ALTHOUGH THERE ARE numerous other ways that can help you build self-esteem; but these are some ways that you can start to augment the level of esteem.

11

DEALING WITH SOCIAL ANXIETY

Social anxiety refers to anxiety or distress in social circumstances. People with social anxiety will consistently feel stupid or humiliated, they will also fear making a terrible impression or being judged by others. For some individuals, social anxiety is restricted to specific sorts of social circumstances.

FOR INSTANCE, a few individuals are extremely uncomfortable in formal work-related circumstances, similar to presentations and gatherings, but do not fear casual gatherings with friends or where socializing is required. Others may demonstrate the careful inverse example, with formal work circumstances being simpler than unstructured get-togethers.

IN REALITY it is a normal phenomenon that a celebrity feels comfortable performing in front huge audience but is shy while interacting with individuals one-on-one or in little gatherings. The amount of social anxiety and the range of dreaded social circumstances fluctuate from individual to individual. For instance, a few individuals experience distress that is reasonable and can be handled, though others are totally overpowered by the force of their fear.

ONE THING that all socially anxious individuals have in common is that they do know that their beliefs are irrational. That is they realize that others are not always assessing or judging them.

THEY COMPREHEND that individuals are not attempting to humiliate or shame them. YET they can't shake it off. With this sort of anxiety, the most causal interaction can seem like a hassle. So if you are experiencing social anxiety, how can you deal with it to effectively interact with woman?

Identify Your Triggers

Social anxiety is not an incurable disease. ACTUALLY there are number of techniques that can help you cope with it. However, the trick is to know which technique might work for YOU. The first step is to get to know your anxiety. This is very important because ONLY when you'll have a better understanding of the problem when you can treat it.

SOCIAL ANXIETY IS different for everyone. Some people might feel anxious in places and situations where they can be judged, whereas others might have a problem when they are asked to share personal thoughts or speak publicly. Once you are able to identify what situation makes you anxious, it will allow you to figure out the best method of treating it. Moreover, you should also note down the symptoms to understand the severity of the problem.

Support Group

Maybe the first thing you ought to be doing with social anxiety issue is attempting to make companions or get closer to the companions you have. Find people who make you feel good and are supportive. These people should be ones who you can share your experiences or converse with.

RESEARCH SUGGESTS that individuals who have a strong support group cope quicker than people who don't have a social network. This is because they feel that they can fall back on their peers or the family and are more open to taking risks.

Practice Relaxation

Relatively few individuals consider stressing as self-programming, yet it is. When you stress strongly over upcoming social circumstances, you will associating anxiety to that particular occasion. At that point when you really go into the social circumstance itself, you feel anxious – you've conditioned yourself to feel along these line.

THESE RESPONSES CAN BE CHANGED if you link the occasion with positive thoughts. Picture yourself as a confident person enjoying the event and your body will eventually form positive link with the event. When you utilize relaxation exercises such as deep breathing, it will help calm physical responses. As a result, you will find it easy to cope with fear, worry and other symptoms.

Consult A Therapist

Irrespective of the popular belief that social anxiety is just being nervous or shy, it is a mental health condition that might need you to get help. Even though, there are a lot of techniques to overcome your anxiety but getting professional help is also imperative.

THESE MENTAL HEALTH experts will be able to guide you about the best technique to use for your particular situation. Moreover, therapy provides a safe environment to run-through anxiety-provoking circumstances. They might also suggest you to join support groups so that you can practice social skills and learn to interact in a positive manner.

Challenging Your Negative Thoughts

People with social anxiety are frequently contemplating how severely things will go bad. For instance, you anticipate that you will fall short of expectations and embarrass yourself. You foresee that everybody will see that you are sweating- - and that they will all discuss about it.

YOU THINK it is a disaster that your brain will go blank. It is vital that you challenge these thoughts and change them into positive ones. You can question yourself to see a clearer picture. "Is it conceivable that individuals don't see you sweating, in light of the fact that they are contemplating what they are going to say?" "Do I have proof that people are discussing me and my anxiety? How would I know?" Reflecting on these negative thoughts will explain how irrationally you have been thinking and it will help you reduce your stress levels.

. . .

AN IMPECCABLE WAY TO deal with social anxiety is to understand the spotlight effect. It will allow you to comprehend that most of the people didn't even notice the blunder you made.

Recognize Your Safety Practices And GET RID Of Them!

People with social anxiety tend to indulge in some safe behaviors that help them conceal their anxiety. They might feel more secure when they use these methods which can include drug use and abuse, dodging eye contact, holding a glass firmly so that other individuals won't see your hands shake, wiping your hands so that individuals won't see you are sweating and talking quick.

THE MORE QUICKLY YOU let go of these practices the more effective your encounters will be—"I did it without a beverage" or "I did it without practicing everything."

Rank Your Fears

The best way to overcome your fears is to set up a hierarchy. List all the events that causes stress and rank them from the least stressful to the most stressful event. You can assign each event a score in terms of the amount of stress caused by each.

AFTER RANKING each of these events, you can practice them. You have to desensitize yourself with each of them. Desensitizing means that you keep experiencing a certain event till you finally stop fearing it. For example if a person fears giving a presentation, the first step to desensitize is to think of presenting.

THE SECOND STEP would be to make a group for presenting. Thirdly, they will have to make a presentation. Fourth step involves preparing for the presentation. Fifth step involves stepping in the hall where presentations are going to take place.

THIS IS GENERALLY KNOWN as the systematic desensitization and it helps a large number of people with their anxiety. Decrease in the level of the anxiety means a decrease the amount of stress experienced.

Avoidance

Many people with social anxiety resort to avoiding stressful situations. However, this will only hamper any progress made. Stop using tactics that help you avoid these situations such as encouraging others to talk more, keeping busy in the kitchen or looking at your phone.

EVEN THOUGH, these behaviors will make you comfortable in the moment; but it will not facilitate you to deal with anxiety. Woman might not reject you but if you do not make an effort to interact with them, then these behaviors won't help. Letting go of these safe practices can be difficult but has a positive long term relationship.

12

TACKLING FACE-TO-FACE INTERACTIONS

W HAT WILL YOU TALK ABOUT ON THE FIRST FEW DATES? Well if you think about this then you are not the only one. Almost everyone who considers dating worries about this, which is why this book will give you a few questions that fit perfectly so you do not have to go through any awkward silences.

FIRST DATES ARE VERY similar to small-scale interviews masked as social outings, whether we like to admit this or not. That is the reason first date questions are so critical and put a lot of pressure.

A FOOLPROOF APPROACH TO guarantee that the conversation will keep flowing is simply ask your date random questions, even though we can never know how agreeable others are with easy-going/casual discussion—that may be easier said than done. The trick is to review effectively a potential suitor on a first date, while at the same time keeping the energy light and fun, and knowing what things to ask and how to ask them.

FOR EXAMPLE, her family, work, pop culture, their hobbies, her favorite music are all surefire bets. There are four things that you should never ask your date when you meet for the first time. That includes information about their exes, politics, religion, and how much they earn in a month.

IF YOU ARE KEEN, you will understand that even the most basic questions can educate you a lot about the person. Here, we have partitioned your theoretical first date into five stages and recommended a progression of things to ask your potential lover amid each stage.

Stage 1: The Initial 10 Minutes

These inquiries are key aspects, the ones to ask after you have said hello, and settled in some place that is comfortable. Although, they are straightforward and boring, yet they will set the tone for your date, and give you immediate things to discuss such as "So, you went to Netherlands? So did my cousin!"

1. What do you do, and how long have you been in this field?

2. Where are you from originally?

3. Where have you had your schooling from?

. . .

4. What was your major?

5. Where precisely do you live in [insert your city or town's name]

Stage 2: After The First Beverage Arrives

Now that you have gotten the basics out of the way, it is time to get a little more particular. Questions over the first beverage ought to be a blend of casual and inquisitive.

THESE QUESTIONS SHOULD ENABLE you to gauge the person's true personality. What are her preferences and dislikes, what do you have in common with each other, the person's hobbies and what they love to do in their spare time?

6. What do you get a kick out of when you are not working or when you have some spare time?

7. Are you a movie person or more of a TV person?

8. Contingent upon the above answer, ask what they have recently watched, or what they have seen of as late.

9. Have you travelled recently? Where to?

10. What kind of music would you say you are into?

. . .

11. Have you read any great books lately?

Stage 3: Things Are Beginning To Get Comfortable

If you and your date are really beginning to like the idea of each other, it is an ideal opportunity to begin slipping in some personal questions, while ensuring neither of you feels constrained to uncover too much.

SOME OF THESE questions might appear silly in the first place, however they can be exceptionally telling. They will likewise assist you both to relax and can prompt some amusing, enthralling discussion.

12. Are you a dog person or a cat person?

13. Do you have any nicknames?

14. In the event that you won the lottery tomorrow, what is the first thing you would purchase?

15. If you are only allowed to eat one thing for the rest of your life, what might it be?

16. Do you have any siblings?

. . .

17. What is your greatest pet peeve?

18. If you could be any individual for a day, who would it be?

19. What do you prefer coffee or tea?

20. Where else would you consider living?

22. Do your folks still live in the house you grew up in?

23. What is on your bucket list?

24. Mornings or night, what do you prefer?

25. Do you ever cook?

26. Do you like your employment? What would you like to do next?

27. Do you consider yourself career-driven?

28. What is your social life like? Do you have a big group of friends?

. . .

29. When is your birthday?

30. What are you most passionate about?

Stage 4: Sign Me Up For A Second Date

Time to seal the deal– the last couple of minutes of a date are essential to guarantee a second date. On the off chance that you think, the date went well; do not be hesitate to let her know. The last question ought to effectively move you out of the date while quietly inferring that you would be down if they want to meet again sometime.

31. Did you like this place?

32. Will I split the check with you? Alright, can I at least leave the tip?

33. Do you have anything exciting planned for the rest of the weekend?

34. How is work looking for you this week?

35. Do you have a bustling week coming up?

36. How are you getting home?

Stage 5: Let's Keep The Date Going

This stage is risky, and should only be reserved if have definite positive strong vibes. In case you are certain, inquire as to whether she would like to proceed with the date somewhere else. Recommend an alternate ending of the night as opposed to just going your different routes after beverages or supper.

37. In the mood for coffee/dessert after this elsewhere?

38. There is this cool bar I know around here, feel like getting a drink?

39. My friend is hosting a get-together a couple blocks away, do you want to stop by?

40. What are we doing after this?

ALL THESE QUESTIONS at different stages will guide you through the process with ease. You are free to ask any other questions that you feel are appropriate according to your situation. These questions are there if you blank out under stress.

ALL YOU NEED to know that the person you are meeting is a human being as well which is why there is no need to stress out.

13

DATING ONLINE

Love is one of the deepest emotions acknowledged by human beings. Similar to other relationships in a person's life, romantic relationships play an imperative role in satisfying our requirements for social connection, intimacy, and sexual relations. Unlike traditional dating, you will not have to visit bars and other social gatherings on a regular basis.

ONLINE DATING or Internet dating is a dating framework that permits people, couples, and groups to reach and correspond with one another through the Internet. The aim behind these conversations and interactions is to indulge in an individual, sentimental, or sexual relationship. Online dating ordinarily gives immoderate matchmaking over the Internet, using cell phones or computers.

IN ORDER TO strike a conversation through this medium, you will have to bring a-game to the table.

. . .

THERE IS a clear distinction between traditional and online dating methods of finding love. You just have to know which one suits you better and where you can possibly find the perfect match. The objective for both the methods is the same and uses the techniques of communicating with another individual to know them better.

THE UTILIZATION of filters is one of the biggest advantages of online dating. You can set these criterions and the algorithm will recommend people who appear to be good matches. These criterions utilize the information added on the profiles or you might have to fill up certain surveys for refined matches. The kind of matches you will receive will obviously depend on the way you created your online profile.

HOWEVER, if you are shy then online dating is the perfect platform for you. The up-side is the anonymity or lack of face to face interaction. This way you can chat online for some time and get comfortable before you actually get to meet the person.

IF YOU DON'T LIKE the way they communicate online; JUST block the URL. You will also not have to deal with the awkwardness that comes with traditional dating.

How Does Online Dating Works?

With online dating, the guidelines of romance and courtship have changed. Relationships in the modern way of dating are complicated. Or so they appear. The rules of traditional dating are not applied anymore, which has left even the most percep-tive of us feeling marginally confused.

DATING today feels hard when it should not be. With the emer-gence of internet and social media, people can now connect with a wider pool of individuals rather than being restricted to their friends, colleagues and people they meet at the bar.

NOW CONCEPTS such as speed dating have emerged and a variety of websites allow you to communicate with a different people to assist you in finding the perfect match. The introduc-tion of dating websites is rising and is not restricted to one particular region or ethnicity. If you are new to the online dating world and are confused about how to communicate with woman through this channel, then this chapter will demon-strate and facilitate you.

YOU WOULD NEED to make a profile on one of the dating sites. The variety of dating sites is humongous, some ask for a membership fee while others are completely free till you want to get a premium package. Steps to date online are outlined below:

CREATE A Profile - in order to create a profile, you will have to put in some basic information such as your name, your gender, your sexual orientation, what gender are you looking for etc. they will also require your birth date and email address so that other members who are interested in you can contact you.

. . .

SOME SITES USE their internal system for people to communicate with one another. If you are very particular about your privacy, you can make a separate email ID specific for your contacts.

DESCRIBE **Physical Attributes** - the next step generally includes describing how you look like such as hair, weight, and body type and eye color. Some sites become more specific and ask for tattoos and piercings. The information at this point becomes very detailed and the sites require you to give more personal questions, such as if you were married, have children etc.

DETAILS **About Your Ideal Date**- then the sites will want you to give information about how you would like your date to be. This information will be used to match you with the perfect fit that is suitable for you. You might get many requests from potential matches from which you can choose from.

POST A PICTURE- POSTING a picture is not always necessary but sites prefer that you do so as research shows an increase in response for profiles that have a picture. Try to make sure that the picture describes you at best and is not a false representation. In addition, your picture should be appropriate to your age.

SELECT AND COMMUNICATE- once you have created a profile and people contact you that is the time you need to be super careful. Do not give personal information in the beginning. Get to know the person first and then decide to meet them. Be cautious and try to meet in a public place.

. . .

CUTTING edge dating has changed the way you meet up with new individuals. Nowadays, singles searching for love regularly employ matchmaking services or make a profile on an internet based dating website in an attempt to find that someone special.

IT IS imperative to have an excellent profile on these sites because the information you add here will basically be your first impression. Looking at these details, a woman will accept or reject your request to engage.

How To Initiate Online Conversations?

Online dating is a new and improved method of meeting the woman of your dreams. Almost everyone is creating online profiles but what do you do after that? There are plenty men aiming to get the same girl as you. How do you initiate?

THE TRICK IS to STAND OUT OF THE CROWD. Naturally, saying things that everyone is saying won't do you any favors. Rather you will just be ANOTHER fish in the pool of prospective lovers. You don't want that now do you? So what can you say to that will get you the attention from the girl of your dream? How do you start a conversation for the girl to notice you?

Compose A Unique Subject Line

You will not believe the number of messages a woman receives. For this reason, you need to have an eye-catching opening message. If the subject line is ridiculous but is catchy, then a woman will read it. Make sure that the subject line of a message is intriguing enough for her to open it and has the basic elements of initiating a conversation.

ONLINE DATING SITES allow you to write subject lines so take advantage. If you neglect this element, chances are that your message will be ignored. Rather than using hey beautiful or similar boring statements, try to be playful and funny.

Do Not Send A Standard Message

Even though it seems like an obvious message to send, but resist the urge to send in basic statements such as hey how are you doing? Instead send in a message that seems personal because it will not look like you have copied and pasted the message. It represents a genuine interest in her.

YOU CAN BEGIN by acknowledging her presence and by thanking them for chatting with you. It will help you initiate the conversation which can be continued by asking questions.

Compliment Her

Unlike meeting face to face, with online dating you will not know the person. You must avoid saying, "you are cute", rather skim through their profile and figure out what attracted you about the woman.

IF IT WAS her smile that drew you to her, then talk about this. It will make her feel special that you noticed the little details rather than using typical one-liners. Do think out of the box. Trust me, it will be appreciated.

Use the Information on the Profile

If you are genuinely interested in a woman, make sure you go through her profile to know what her likes and dislikes are. A majority of the men tend to neglect this element when it comes to online dating.

THIS CAN EASILY LEAD to rejection and disappointment. Each dating site will have you make a profile. It is there for a reason: TO HELP YOU KNOW THE OTHER PERSON'S DETAILS. The profile offers a sneak peek into a woman's life. Even though women tend to conceal the details on their profile but there is always some information that can be used to initiate a conversation.

Provide Details

Now that you have already given a compliment and have skimmed through her profile, make sure you come across as an interesting person as well. This is the only way you can ensure to get a response. When you write traveling on your profile, make sure you expand on it. Otherwise, it will only seem that you are making it up.

WHEN CONVERSING WITH HER, talk about your travel experiences as it will allow you to talk about more things. Thus, it will be a representation that you are genuinely interested in her.

Do Not Keep Mentioning That You Are New To Online Dating.

If you keep talking about how new you are to the dating world and are confused how it works, then it only shows your lack of confidence. No one cares! This is just a bring topic and it will only make the woman awkward.

REMEMBER that you are trying to date a woman. You are not hiring her as an instructor to guide you through online dating sites. The plan is to charm and impress her enough to keep the conversation going. Similarly, you must not ask her about how long she has been using these platforms.

Don't Act Cool

Being cocky and acting who you are not is a major turn-off. You should use words that show vulnerability and kindness. The ultimate goal is to communicate with a woman enough to make her want to meet you in person.

YOU MUST NOT BE TOO shy or too aggressive when conversing with a woman. If you act or find it difficult to keep up with the conversation, chances are that a woman will catch that instantly.

Incorporate Teasing

Some light hearted teasing is a great way to show your fun-loving side. This is a highly attractive quality and is appreciated by women. It allows you to dig deeper about a person in a causal manner. Moreover, it displays positivity that will make a woman want to meet you. No one prefer the company of a negative individual.

Positive men exude confidence and seem sure of their future, which attracts a woman towards them. This quality will make you stand out and will also give you a kick start to having an interesting conversation.

Be Brief

When chatting online, avoid writing long messages about what you enjoy and the things you dislike. Imagine someone coming up to you and start listing their favorite podcasts. Would you like it? we don't think so.

Talking about your hobbies and interests is a great communication starter, however, talking endlessly about yourself can be boring. Women love to talk and want the man to listen carefully. For this reason, you should be concise and allow the woman to do most of the talking. She will appreciate it as they pour their heart out.

Ultimate Goal: Meet the Woman in Person

At the end of the day, your goal should be to meet the person face to face. To make this happen, stop dragging the conversation and ask for her number. It will increase your chances to meet with her.

It is essential to remember that pushing her to meet too soon will only lead to a chaotic situation. Unless you had a pen pal in mind, you must gather the courage and ask for her number. With online dating, the possibilities are unlimited.

However, it all comes down to having a high-quality and detailed profile so that the algorithms can match you with a woman who is highly compatible with you. Having a comprehensive profile will allow you to eliminate women who have different interests.

14

TEXTING QUESTIONS / TOPICS TO KEEP THE CONVERSATION GOING

W hen you are out with your guy friends, you have plenty to talk about, right? Topics such as sports, music, movies etc. are regular things to discuss. BUT when you go out with a woman, some men might find it difficult to converse. Their brain might freeze or they go blank. There are couples of reasons for experiencing this mind numbing situation including a lack of confidence, anxiety, or even nerves.

TO AVOID SUCH SITUATIONS, it is best to have a list of questions or topics up your sleeves. It will allow you to look confident, which ultimately leads to a successful interaction.

Topics to Discuss

Having a list of topics to talk about with a woman on the safe side can transform a normal conversation to something way more delightful. It will allow you to keep the conversation smooth rather than running into awkward breaks.

. . .

WHETHER YOU ARE on the first date or getting to know a person through an online platform, these topics can ensure that the conversation does not get stalled.

MUSIC

WHO DOESN'T LIKE MUSIC? This is an excellent topic to keep the conversation going even over text. However, this does not mean that you should list your top favorite albums. Rather enquire the genre she loves listening to and talk about that. In case she is not into something you like, bite the urge to get aggressive.

Future Plans

EVEN THOUGH, it might seem like a topic that is bought up in an interview. However, you can get creative and phrase the question in a way that allows you to dig deep. Stay focused on your life in general rather than talking about where you see yourself working in the next few years. You can drop in the idea of having kids in the future and see her stance on this notion.

FOOD

WITH AN EXTENSIVE RANGE of cuisines accessible in the market, chances are that the woman of your dreams does have a favorite. Whether it's Chinese or sushi, asking about this is a great way to keep the conversation going. In addition, it will allow you to plan a date at her favorite eatery.

PERSONAL STRUGGLES

ONCE YOU HAVE GOTTEN to know the woman a little better, then introducing some deep topics is an excellent way to connect. You can share the struggles you have experienced and enquire about theirs. This will automatically build a bond.

HOWEVER, you will have to be careful. Do not let the conversation get sour. Rather, steer it in the direction that will help her build trust and a deep emotional association.

ETHICS

WHEN YOU ARE GETTING to know a woman, conversations might seem never ending. After a couple of texting days, you might observe a dying conversation. In these moments, you can introduce some questionable topics such their beliefs about morally problematic systems and ideas.

IT COULD INCLUDE topics such as racism, slavery, wage rates etc. It is crucial that you sense the tone after introducing this idea. If the woman is reluctant to talk about this, then ditch the topic.

. . .

DREAMS

NOT EVERYONE WILL BE comfortable to talk about their dreams. But if the woman you are conversing with seems interested, then this can be an awesome topic. When you talk about a person's goals and dreams, it will give you insight into what they wish to achieve in life. People love talking about it unless they are stuck and can't figure out their passions.

Intriguing Questions To Ask Over Text

Even though, you might be a smooth talker but it is best to have a couple of questions in the back pocket just in the case the spark dies down. Whether you just met a girl in the bar or you have known her for a while, it is imperative to ask questions that are meaningful. This way it will show her that you are interested and not playing around. These questions should be able to facilitate you in knowing the person better and direct towards a deeper connection.

WHAT'S YOUR NAME?

FIRSTLY, you obviously need to ask them their name. However, if you got in touch with them through social media platforms then chances are that you already know their name. Getting the introductions out of the way in the beginning can make you avoid the embarrassment of calling her other names. Listen carefully so that you do not forget her name.

What Are You Passionate About These Days?

Have you ever noticed that a particular topics excites the person you are talking to? If so, then you might have introduced a topic that they are passionate about or something that inspires them.

Ask a woman about their passions and you will find them excitedly talking it that subject for hours. Moreover, it generates a positive feeling, which she will associate with you later on. If you can make your love interest talk about their passions, it will do wonders for your relationship.

What Are Your Hidden Talents?

When you ask this question, remember that the term talent is subjective. Different people might see a particular skill as talent because they might be exceptionally good at it. Make sure that you do not judge a woman when they talk about their hidden talents.

People might have talents including playing an instrument, juggling, or even singing opera. Once you discover their talents, it can initiate interesting related topics.

How Often Do You Travel? (Do You Enjoy Traveling?)

This question is good for two reasons: it will allow you to see the compatibility. For example, if you love to travel but the woman prefers to stay home rather than take adventurous trips; then the compatibility is low.

· · ·

MOREOVER, it will help you steer the conversations in the future. If you and the woman have travelled a lot, it will allow you to share your travel stories. In case that she hasn't travelled a lot but would love to; then you can be a virtual guide.

Which Fictional Character Can You Relate With?

Asking this question will tell you how the woman sees herself and will allow you to understand her personality. Does the woman of your dreams identify with Monica from Friends or Khaleesi from Game of Thrones? You can also have a cheesy reply for such questions. Respond over text by saying "Does that make me your Chandler?" Remember to have a humorous reply to these questions as it will allow you to stand out.

What's Your Stance On The Pineapple Pizza Dialogue?

Try to make your conversations intriguing and something that builds curiosity. In a latest trend, people have been debating over pineapple pizza on the Internet. Ask her opinion on this delicious topping. It will keep her interested and excited to offer her opinion.

How Do You Celebrate Your Birthday?

Asking her about her date of birth and the way she celebrates is also an interesting question. It will allow you find her date of birth and another chance to hang out. Moreover, you can ask whether she loves a quiet night with friends or goes wild partying and celebrating this important day. As a result, you will be able to plan a birthday accordingly.

. . .

WHEN IT COMES to choosing a backup topic, the sky is the limit. Just steer your conversation to topics and questions that intrigue you and your partner.

15

SIGNS THAT SHE IS NOT INTO YOU

The most difficult things anyone can experience is not receiving reciprocity from the person you love. Unrequited love is terrible and painful. When a woman does not love you back, the feeling of rejection can be crushing.

IN SUCH SITUATIONS, men either feel humiliated or just go in denial. The latter stage is way more dangerous because you will start reading into little signs of praise and affection a woman sends towards you.

AT THE END of the day, you will only be delaying the heartbreak and its acceptance. Remember you cannot force anyone to love you back. This is just a harsh reality that you have to accept.

THE SOONER YOU REALIZE IT, the easier it will be for you to move on. So if you want to avoid the heartbreak and embarrassment, then look for these signs that indicate she might not be into you:

She Wants To Keep You In The Friend Zone

If a woman keeps forcing that your relationship with them is platonic, then there is a high chance that she is not interested in dating you. Moreover, when a woman keeps referring to you as a friend and explicitly introduces you this way, then you need to get the hint because she is trying to tell you something.

EVEN THOUGH, it hurts but you should be mindful of your reaction. It is imperative to avoid throwing a fit. You should be grateful that she is offering you her friendship. If you force your feelings on her, you will lose a good friend. In case, it is difficult for you to be friends with the woman you love; just move on.

Does Not Initiate Meet Ups

If a woman does not plan to meet up or initiate it, then she might not be as interested to go on a date with you. Reflect on it: if she really liked you, then she would invite you to see a new movie release or when going to see a play. When a woman does not make plans with you, it is a clear signs that her interests lie elsewhere.

MOREOVER, she might try to change the topic when you try and make plans. She might say things like "I would like to stay single for a while". Sometimes, a woman might accept the offer to go on a date but might leave early to circumvent any romantic gestures at the end of the date.

. . .

IN SUCH CIRCUMSTANCES, you should stop making efforts because you deserve someone who loves you back. Another sign is that she flakes on the plans by calling in sick or saying that she is busy.

Replying To Messages

Another sign that a woman is not interested in you romantically is when they take hours or days to respond to a text. No one is so busy that they cannot take out the time to reply to a single text. Not responding in time only shows their lack of interest.

MOREOVER, even when they reply the messages sent will have no emotion or enthusiasm to continue. It is a clear indication that she is talking to you forcefully, so relieve her of this painful situation.

Giving Silly Excuses and Lies

Some women just aren't looking for a partner yet, maybe because they do not want a commitment or they might just be busy developing their career. In this modern and fast paced world, women are as busy as men.

IF A WOMAN DOES NOT RESPOND, then they might have overcommitted or just don't want to date right now. When a woman starts to give you silly excuses or false information, then you should put your energy elsewhere.

Moves Away On Physical Contact

Constant touching is an indication of a romantic gesture. These include playful hitting, touching the arms and the legs or even stroking the hair. When a woman does not indulge in these activities and has a stiff and unapproachable body language, then she might be trying to tell you something.

YOUR CRUSH MIGHT BE GIVING you subtle information that she is not interested in a romantic relationship. It is crucial that you read these signs clearly because an unsolicited touch is invasive and creepy. An absence of physical contact exhibits that a woman might just want to be your friend.

Doesn't Make The Effort To Dress Up

Irrespective of whether you are a tomboy or super feminine, majority of women do make an effort to get all dolled up prior to a date. Every woman is different, which implies that the extent of dressing up is dependent on their personality. Some girls might prefer wearing a slightly tighter jeans while others might match their bags and shoes.

IN SHORT, when you a woman knows that their crush will be around; they do dress up. If a woman isn't making the extra effort to clean up, then there is a high chance that she is not interested in you.

16

HOW TO START A CONVERSATION?

E nquire from a woman about what they look in a man and she will most likely say confidence, intelligence, and a sense of humor; among numerous other aspects. Knowing how to initiate a conversation with a woman exhibits that you have all that she is searching without having to brag or list all your finest traits.

ONCE YOU RECOGNIZE how to begin a conversation with a woman you will have all the aids to put your greatest foot forward and make her wish for more and more time with you.

ACTUALLY, an excellent first conversation tends to increase your chances that a girl will say yes to the date or maybe a drink. This will allow you to continue to display your best qualities. Although corny pickup lines will get a girl's attention but this does not keep the conversation going. Some of the effective ways to initiate an interesting conversation are:

Introduce Yourself

Naturally, the first step to ignite a conversation (whether face-to-face or over text) is by introducing yourself. There are creative ways to introduce yourself which will allow you to remain mysterious as well.

INTRODUCTIONS ARE imperative because you do not want the girl to not be able to reach you or contact you later one. Staying a stranger with the person you like defeats the purpose of all the efforts.

Be Very Clear About Your Intentions

Who likes a conversation that is going nowhere? If you continue to beat around the bush, then chances are you will miss a perfect opportunity. Not being able to talk straight is a child's play. Act like a man and talk in a manner that clarifies your intentions. If you have a love interest then shows it through your body language.

WHEN THE CONVERSATION is going in a positive direction, then you can explicitly state that you wish to take her to a dinner, a movie, or even skiing to the nearest resort. This will solely depend on what you can afford and your personality. Just ask her. What's the worst that can happen?

Ask Questions

If you aren't exactly good at making conversation, then your best bet is on asking open ended questions. This is because a close ended question will only result in a Yes or No answer. On the contrary, an open-ended question employs when, what, how, where, and why questions.

MOREOVER, this elicits opinions, feelings and thoughts. A better technique is to devise a list of at least 5 to 10 questions that you can ask. Make sure that they are general such as sports, politics, or a hobby.

YOU MUST AVOID TALKING about ex-husbands, boyfriends, money and even horrible friends. Also be open to listening and hearing contradictory opinions.

Allow Silence

If you feel like you are stalling or running out of interesting topics, then you can try to be silent for a moment. Majority of the times, people get uncomfortable in silence, but you must show her that you are relaxed sitting silently and not focused on filling these gaps. This also gives her time to breathe and consider what she wants to discuss.

MOREOVER, listening will only happen when you stop talking. Put in a question and listen. It is the formula for a great date.

Give Her a Meaningful Compliment

If the talk takes a normal break, take an instant to give her an honest compliment. You do not have to look desperate and keep talking about her eyes or her hair, however you can tell her that you like the dress she is wearing or the way she laughs is just amazing.

. . .

WHEN YOU PRAISE a girl you retain the conversation and it is easy to carry it on. Moreover, you get bonus points for paying consideration to the way she is. You may also want to give her recommendation but make sure you leave arrogance out of it.

Conversational Tips To Talk To Women

Learning how to effectively communicate with a woman is an essential skill that every man should master especially when they are looking for a long term relationship. Although it isn't always easy to converse with a woman and every man isn't born with skills to communicate smoothly; however, mastering these skills isn't impossible.

ALL IT REQUIRES IS a little practice and figuring out a couple of tips that can facilitate you to make stimulating conversation.

WOMEN LOVE to have intelligent conversation, prefer empathy and genuineness. Incorporate all these elements in the way you converse, and you will be successful in appealing the girl of your dreams. Moreover, when talking to a woman nerves also play a major role. It is imperative to know what will keep you calm or how you can come across to be confident.

LET'S look at some of the conversational tips that can help you converse with women effectively:

Focus On Her!

Never let your anxieties and the fear of rejection stop you from approaching a woman. If she chooses to say no or not respond altogether; then it could be about her. For instance, she might not be looking for a relationship or have her own insecurities.

WHEN YOU ARE CONSTANTLY FOCUSING on what you must say next; the woman of your dream will pick up on that. You will not be able to grasp 100% of her attention. This is simply because you will be focused on yourself. Basically if you both will be listening to the voices in your head; then naturally you aren't exactly paying attention to each other or what the other person is saying.

Allow The Woman To Talk About Herself

A successful conversation is one where both the parties have an equal chance to talk. For this reason, an essential conversational tip is to be a good listener and keep track of the topics being discussed so that you can have an appropriate response.

THIS IS PRETTY simple and gives you a break to stop coming up with brilliant questions. For instance, if you begin a conversation by giving a compliment about their scarf or jewelry and the woman responds by saying that their mom gave it to them.

THEN YOU CAN SAY "What a wonderful mother you have". Make sure you smile along with the comment. You can be creative and say something that the other person will agree with. You do need to resist the urge to talk about yourself consistently.

. . .

MAKE IT ABOUT HER. Keeping the conversation flowing and listening to her will facilitate the process of becoming friends with her. After that, you can easily invite her for coffee without looking like a creep.

Utilize Conversation Threading

Conversation threading is a method through which you can use another person's statement to extract a couple of topics. These topics will help you continue the discussion further. For instance, "if the woman talks about how they had to travel for their job", then pick up on that.

BRING up traveling in general and share some of your adventures. You might also ask questions about how their trip was or questions related to the particular area. Another topic that can emerge from this is about their job. The possibilities are unlimited.

Practice Makes Perfect

Even though this might seem silly and obvious, but it is something that people ignore. Similar to every other area in life, practicing the art of communicating smoothly is no different.

YOU CAN PRACTICE CONVERSING with friends, family and salesmen at the grocery store. Another interesting arena are the online platforms. Hone your skills through online chats and try avoiding the use of webcams.

Say What You Are Thinking

It does not mean that should blurt out EVERYTHING such as "your bag does not match your clothes" or "those pants are ugly". Look around and you will notice that smooth talkers are those people who are not constantly thinking about what to say next or whether people will judge them on what they are saying. These individuals are uninhibited and are confident in what they say.

IF YOU ARE LOOKING to converse with women in the best way, then utilize this technique. You do not have to mention every stupid thing that comes to your mind. Just create a flow in the conversation without over thinking it. Simply bring up an interesting topic and keep the conversation going.

Don't Intrude Upon Personal Space

Part of giving respect to a woman is making sure that you aren't crossing any lines or giving her ample space. When you move in very close to a woman, she might start to feel uncomfortable and that will put a halt to the conversation instantly.

WHEN YOU VIOLATE limits in the first meeting, it sets a precedence that you will do the same in the future.

Make Sure You End The Conversation In Time

This is literally the most important step because if you keep the conversation going for too long, you might end up boring the woman. Although it might be difficult to tell the right time to end a conversation if it is going great, but remember that it's always better to end the conversation earlier.

IT WILL ALLOW you and the other person to have something to talk when you meet the next time. Naturally, you should wait for the right moment rather than interrupting the other person abruptly. Even though, it might be difficult to know EXACTLY when to stop talking, however you must try to end it on a positive note. It is imperative to get some contact information (whether through social media platforms or a phone number) and give them a clear hint that you would like to meet again.

17

WHAT IF THE CONVERSATION IS STALLING?

People all over the world are now shifting to online platforms to find their soul mate. However, with emotions and facial expressions lacking during online chats or texting; the conversation might die out sooner than you expected. Texting is an excellent method of communicating and keeping in touch but it comes with some challenges.

So WHAT CAN you do if the conversation seems like it's dying but you still want to keep talking? You can try a wide range of techniques to keep the conversation going. Boost it by circling back to a topic that sparked joy or maybe introduce a new subject. Try the methods mentioned below if your text conversation is stalling:

"What Is Your Opinion About...?"

Kick start the conversation by enquiring her opinion on an event or product. People love sharing their opinions regarding things that they have used or adventures they would love to go on. Utilize this tactic and ask a question that will encourage a woman to articulate their opinion and express what they really think.

AVOID BRINGING up topics that are controversial such as religion or politics. It is particularly true for text conversations because the other person won't be able to catch your tone, which might lead to an undesirable outcome.

POSE the question in a light mood. For instance, you can say something like," I have a serious question for you. Eggs, French toast or waffles? Be honest."

Flattery And Compliments

Another interesting method of keeping the conversation going is by using flattery or complimenting the woman about something they own or the way they dress. This is a sure shot way to pick up a dying conversation because you can never go wrong by pointing out something nice.

YOU CAN SLIP in a compliment in the middle of your conversation or talk about a quality that you have always admired. Compliments whether they are casual, encourage people to open up. Statements such as "you have a beautiful smile that brightens my day", or "you give me the best advice" will not only make people feel good, but it also encourages them to talk more.

. . .

ANOTHER INTERESTING TRICK is to ask them a question and compliment them. For example, you can say where did you buy that cool too you were wearing the other day? Such statements will bring the magic back to your dying conversations.

Introduce A Blast From The Past

A major chunk of a person's personality is formed in their childhood. If the conversation is dying, ask them "When you were a kid, did you...?." This is the best way to ignite the dying sparks of a conversation. It also allows you to discover interesting things about their childhood.

IT IS a great strategy when you are texting with someone you feel comfortable with. Bring in questions that will make them talk about their hobbies and activities as a child. It will give you insight into their family background, their beliefs and the kind of environment they were raised in. However, there is a risk attached to this method. Childhood memories can also bring about emotional moments to the surface.

IF A WOMAN GETS upset or seems to be touchy regarding s topic; avoiding prying or digging deep. Questions about the past should include light conversations. You can ask about their favorite vacation spot or the Disney Princess she adored etc.

Ask For Movie Or Season Recommendations

Want to keep the light conversation mood going? Ask them about what they are watching these days. This can also be branched out to other entertainment arenas such as what the woman of your dreams is reading, listening and watching.

.   .   .

THE CONVERSATION CAN THEN GO in two directions. Either you have already watched that series or you are clueless about it. Either ways you can keep the conversation going. If you haven't watched or heard a particular podcast; you can ask them to tell you a bit more.

IN CASE A WOMAN brings up that they have been listening to podcasts or started reading, you can say that you have been looking to start reading. Where can you begin? Or if she has some recommendations?

Create Suspense

Statements such as " you can never guess ..." are bound to create curiosity and will draw the person to keep the conversation going. This is a great tactic because it will leave the person thinking what will come next.

WHEN YOU MAKE statement such as guess what I saw or who I ran into, make sure the follow-up answer is strong enough to not disappoint the woman. Saying things like 'the funniest thing happened at work' will show them that you were thinking about them during the event.

Show Interest

If you sense that the conversation is dying and remembers an interesting topic that was talked about early on; bring it up again. Circle back to a topic that the woman of your dream seemed interested in.

. . .

You can say "tell me more about ..." It will show them that you were paying attention and that you are a good listener. For example, if the woman says that they can't decide what to have for dinner, you can ask "so what did you end up ordering?" "Did you enjoy the meal?"

Think About Old Times

You can also breathe life into the conversation by telling a funny story that involves both of you or even a joke. This will bring a smile to the person's face and they might also remember something relatable.

Going down the memory lane can be a beautiful journey especially when you both have shared a lot of moments together. You might also come with an inside joke that you both had. For example, it could be a person dressed eccentrically or maybe something that the waiter said. It is imperative to bring up something that you both thought was funny.

Make sure that it's not something that was embarrassing for her. If your relationship is new and there are no funny stories to reminisce, then you can share a relatable meme.

18

IMPROVING COMMUNICATION SKILLS

Communication is a buzzword and everyone seems to be improving this skill: whether for a better interpersonal relationship or to improve their work environment. The importance of communication is pressed upon with a good reason: it helps us enjoy a life without misunderstandings and allows for a greater level of joy.

HOWEVER, just reading and hearing about it isn't enough. You will have to absorb all the information and use it in your distinct situation. It is particularly true for individuals who struggle with proper communication skills.

EVERYONE HAS the innate ability to talk and communicate smoothly. If you want to improve your communication skills or are curious how to do so, then you are in the right place. This segment of the book talks about the areas that require attention while improving communication and the ways that you can augment these skills.

Four Main Areas for Improvement

Effective communication is imperative whether you are going to interview for a job or want to work on your interpersonal skills. If you are looking to learn the best areas that show visible improvement, then delve on these four major communication areas. These areas of improvement are emotional awareness, the way you question, non-verbal communication and listening.

EMOTIONAL MANAGEMENT and Awareness

PEOPLE TEND to ignore this aspect of communication but having the awareness of your emotions and the ability to read other person's emotions is a crucial skill. Once you are aware of the emotions, it becomes a lot easier to manage them.

EVEN WHEN YOU are working or interacting with others in life, everything that comes your way can't be handled logically. There are number of situations that require emotional decisions. Leaving your emotions at home is never an option or a wise decision.

WHEN YOU ARE aware of positive and negative emotions; it will allow you to improve communication. Tapping into emotional intelligence is crucial to survive now and is now considered an important dominator for your overall success.

· · ·

EMOTIONAL INTELLIGENCE HAS an extensive range of components that are segmented into social and personal skills. Part of the social skills include meeting others, empathy etc. Factors such as motivation, self-awareness and self-regulation.

SELF-AWARENESS AND EMPATHY are ranked highly important. Being empathetic implies to the ability to understand and feel what others are going through. The main idea is to improve the skills and master the way you manage your emotions around others. It will allow you to work well with one another and facilitate in developing deeper connections.

LISTENING INTENTLY

IN ORDER TO improve your communication abilities, you must listen carefully. Humans tend to forget that conversations should be on both ends. We have a tendency of either talking about ourselves or only telling your story.

THIS WAY you will not listen to what others have to say. Another common behavior pattern that is seen when communicating with others is thinking about what to say next rather than actively participating in the conversation.

WOMEN ARE talkative beings and they love a smooth talker. If you are looking for improvement, then try to polish your listening skills. BUT there is a difference between hearing and listening. Learning to listen intently implies that you pay attention to the words that are spoken along with how they are conveyed.

MOREOVER, it means that you observe the non-verbal messages that are transmitted. To sum it up, listening means that you give your undivided attention to the person you are conversing with and concentrate on what they are saying. There are some excellent techniques that are utilized by good listeners.

THESE INCORPORATE REFLECTION and clarification as to what the person said, which allows them to avoid misunderstandings. When you use these techniques, it shows that other person that you are genuinely listening.

READING And Comprehending Non-Verbal Cues

DID YOU KNOW THAT 80% of our communication is through non-verbal communication? Looking at these statistics, it is only true to consider reading and understanding this form of communication. It is typically considered that ONLY body language makes up non-verbal communication; however, there are numerous other aspects as well.

THESE INCLUDE EYE CONTACT, facial expressions, pitch of your voice, posture and body movement. Some physiological changes are also considered as nonverbal communication such as sweating.

. . .

WHEN YOU PAY attention to these signs of communication, it will allow you to better understand the message that the other person is trying to convey. Moreover, you will be able to convey your message clearly by ensuring consistency in body language and words.

HONE YOUR QUESTIONING Skills

THE LAST AREA that can be improved for betterment in communication is your ability to ask questions. It is something that a number of people struggle with. When you ask questions, it shows that you are listening carefully and understand what the other person is trying to say.

MOREOVER, it allows you to get further and in depth information about a topic. Asking the right questions will also help in keeping the conversation going. People who are good listeners are also great at asking questions because they try to extract information rather than share their own opinions.

WAYS OF IMPROVING Communication Skills

COMMUNICATION SKILLS CAN BE DIVIDED into three separate and clear segments. Each of these is imperative and play a vital role in defining who you are and how well you can communicate to build relationships and to maintain them. The three types of communications are: verbal, non-verbal and written.

. . .

WRITTEN communication is also gaining precedence now given that online dating and texting is on the rise. Websites such as tinder, Facebook messenger and other social media platforms require the use of written communication to interact with acquaintances, lovers or even friends. It tends to be the hardest given that written communication does not incorporate tone of voice, pitch etc.

WITH VERBAL COMMUNICATION, you can easily take note of the factors that need to be modified and alter them. Face to face communication improvements come in the form of confidence and self-esteem developments. Non-verbal communication can be altered by making changes in the posture, controlling your eye movements and facial expressions.

ALL THE TIPS and tricks mentioned below will cater to three types of communication. Read, absorb and apply these tips so that you can improve your communication skills:

Be Brief And Clear

Have you ever heard a story that is long with EXTRA details that you lose track? Other people feel the same way. So when you are conversing, it is essential to keep your story short, interesting and limit the details to the ones that are important.

ONE WAY TO achieve this is by getting to the main part of your point or story so that people actually listen.

Try To Avoid Assumptions

Communication skills can seriously be hampered if you keep assuming things on your end. When you assume things such as "I know what they want", it will only lead to misunderstandings. These little things can escalate and become a major conflict.

FOR THIS REASON, active listening is a vital component for improving communication skills. Moreover, communicating also requires you to be empathetic so that you can change the direction of the conversation if the woman you are talking to feels uncomfortable. You will need to develop this skill because sometimes people say things that they don't actually mean.

THIS USUALLY ENSUES in a complex situation where a person might get overwhelmed or humiliated. In these situations, people tend to hide their real emotions or needs. When you enquire about something, listen carefully so that any misunderstandings can be minimized. In addition, it decreases the risk of conflict.

Stay Comfortable With Silence

Some people get super uncomfortable when there is silence. However, it's good to allow silence once in a while. If you keep talking, chances are that you will start to blabber details that are boring, unimportant or something that might leave a bad impression.

.   .   .

ALTHOUGH IT IS DIFFICULT, but you must fight the urge because it leads to effective communication. If you keep talking, the actual message is generally lost. As a result, you or the other person does not communicate effectively or remember each other's message.

Avoid Using "Uh's" And "Umm's"

Even though it might seem like common sense, but think about the last conversation you had. How many fillers did you use? A lot. If you give a presentation, try and record it. Listen to it later on and see how often you use these fillers.

ONCE YOU TAKE note of the frequency, then stay alert in your next conversations. The best idea is to speak slowly so that you have time to think about what to say.

Bridge The Gap When Changing Topic

Need to change the topic of discussion during a conversation? Master it by altering the topic tactfully. You will have to be observant and locate a common denominator that will link the conversation from where it is now to where you want to steer it. Using connecting phrases is an excellent idea when changing the topic. These phrases include, "here is what I know.." or "I believe.." etc.

Learn Soft Skills

Even though technical skills might be imperative when you are working. However, when conversing with a woman, it is essential to have a good grip on soft skills. These incorporate abilities such as teamwork, adaptability, empathy and having an open mind.

ALL THESE ASPECTS come together and have a direct impact on improving the quality of your communication. Development of soft skills will ensure effective conversations.

Do Not Show A Power Pose

A power pose is when you stand with your arms crossed. It can come across as a rude gesture however, this is a common sign of being defensive. It represents that you are guarded or feeling uncomfortable.

IT ALSO DISPLAYS that you want to get out of the conversation as soon as you can. This posture will naturally hinder the conversation rather than improving this skill. For this reason, you must ensure a good posture.

Formal Vs. Informal Writing

When it comes to written communication, the person you are conversing with will determine your style of communication. For example, when texting a woman you can utilize informal language or acronyms. However, when writing professional emails; it is best to avoid words such as "Hey" or "BRB."

ANOTHER CONSIDERATION TO keep in mind when communicating in this manner is whether or not the other person knows what these acronyms are. For this reason, it is vital that you alter your communication style according to the person you are conversing with.

Always Proofread

During written communications, individuals generally believe that there are no mistakes in the draft. This is especially true when conversing with a lover, where you just want to press send as quickly as possible.

WHEN CHATTING with a lover or writing a work email, it is crucial that you do not rush. Make sure you read the draft prior to sending for any mistakes. Remember that spotting mistakes in your writing might be tough when checked right after finishing the draft. One tip is to take a break, and proofread it.

HOWEVER, while chatting you might have to respond right way. Type slowly so that you have time to think what you want to say next.

Words And Sentences Should Be Simple

When texting or chatting online, make sure that your sentences are not very long. A general rule suggests that a sentence should be less than two lines. Try to make shorter but clear statements and cut the sentence in half where you can.

IT IS ALSO essential to avoid using difficult words or over complicating the structure of the sentence. Big words might be difficult to understand or you might not use them correctly.

Keep A Check On Your Tone

Majority of miscommunication ensues because one or both the parties had an inappropriate tone of voice that did not correspond with the environment or the overall circumstances.

WHEN TALKING TO A WOMAN, try to have a balanced tone (not too loud and not too soft) of the parties involved was not speaking in the right tone. Don't be too loud, don't be too soft, and don't be rude or condescending. Always communicate politely and respectfully with everyone.

Do Not Respond When You Are Upset

Last but the most important tip to improve your communication while texting is to never respond when you are mad or frustrated. If you do come across an upsetting email or message, take a walk and cool yourself before replying. You do not want to say something so hurtful that it becomes difficult to mend the relationship.

19

TIPS TO AVOID FRIEND ZONE

E veryone in this world has a label associated with them. For someone who is looking for love and a partner, the friend zone is a frightening tag to have. It is because after you have been locked there, you will not have a quick escape.

WHEN YOU ARE HOPING for a relationship with a woman, it is imperative to make the right move from the point you approached them till the end.

FLIRTING in the right way and altering you initial moves will facilitate you to avoid the friend zone altogether. However in the off-chance you do get friend zoned by a girl, it doesn't mean that you are stuck in this state permanently.

TO AVOID GOING through this agony, follow the tips below so that you can relieve yourself from the suffering.

. . .

HERE ARE some methods that can help you avoid the friend zone:

Learn To Be Mysterious

We understand that all humans love to talk about themselves. However, if you blurt everything out in the first meeting then there won't be any excitement left. Staying mysterious is very attractive for women and it will make them want to prolong the conversation. Keep some cards in your hands.

WHEN YOU TELL everything in the first meeting, it shows that you are needy and desperate. A mysterious man will make a woman curious and a challenge will keep them interested. It will make them think about you and would want to dig deeper. For all the reasons mentioned, you should maintain a balance regarding what you ought to share.

Stop Being The Best Friend Or The Nice Guy

Acting like a nice guy or slipping into the best friend role can seem like an easy choice as these are trustworthy roles without any complications. However, once you are in the friend zone coming out of it can be tough.

MOREOVER, it becomes difficult to express your real feelings without putting your friendship at a risk. Stop being someone that you are not. Learn to take a stand and try to get rid of labels that hinder your love life.

. . .

YOU CAN GET out of the friend zone by gaining confidence and being true to yourself. Use body language cues to tell your friend that you like them and you are interested in them (not just as friends).

Make Romantic Gestures

Owing to the fear of losing already existing friendships, people tend to make the mistake of acting like a friend. In order to avoid such situations, you should display romantic gestures.

IF YOU KEEP ACTING like a friend, a woman will not get the hint that you are interested in them. When you show romantic interest, a woman will pick up on it and might reciprocate. Romantic gestures are one of the best ways to show someone that you love them and want to be more than just friends. It is an old fashioned technique to show someone that you care.

Be Consistent But Not Clingy

The key to avoiding friend zone is balance amongst all other things in life. Being too clingy or not being there after a phase of good time will only confuse the woman on your stance. If you leave the person with no information or disappear on them, it will make them unsure of your feelings.

IT IS ALSO true for conversations through texting. Showing signs of text anxiety or not replying for a day will also lead to the same outcome. If you are looking to stay out of the friend zone, ensure that your texting phase is lively and healthy.

. . .

EVEN THOUGH BEING consistent is imperative, it does not mean that you should cling on to her. A significant step is to give space. In addition, look for signs of discomfort (if any) and reorganize the way you move forward.

Jealousy Doesn't Always Help

There are some relationships that can be helped by making the other person jealous. However, if you are looking to avoid the friend zone; then this technique isn't always advised. It is better to keep calm and learn ways that can make a woman trust you.

WHEN YOU EXHIBIT signs of jealousy and insecurity, it weakens the relationship as it is considered to be a negative response. All you can do is play your part well, express your feelings and treat them right. If all these efforts do not work, then it just wasn't worth it. Accept the fact that she might not like you and no one can force feelings of love on to another person.

Gentle Touches Go a Long Way

Once you have started to see the girl on a more consistent basis, retain the flirtation behavior. This is the most effective way to show them that you are interested in more than just friendship with them.

NEVER TRY this with a stranger especially at a social situation such as a bar. But you can gently touch a woman you are romantically involved with or know her at least. Resting your arm around her shoulder, holding her hand when helping her get up are some ways you can touch her appropriately; yet it is gentle. This is a powerful technique and these touches can create a difference.

Have a Strong Alpha Body Language

Men generally like to pretend that they are far more brave compared to the reality. Having a strong Alpha Body Language might mean aggressiveness or showing power to men; but for women the term "alpha male" has different characteristics. When you are taking a woman out on a date; look from their perspective.

HERE HAVING an Alphas male body language doesn't imply that you act like an arrogant individual. Rather it defines an excellent posture, a great sense of humor, and a body language that is all about confidence. For instance, open your chest and stand tall. You may also want to keep your hands behind to exhibit openness.

MOREOVER, the impression is also in the handshake. This shouldn't be too flimsy neither too hard and do not forget to smile.

Play Hard to Get

Women also love the chase. If you are accessible too easily, it will not give them the room to crave for you. For this reason, it is a good idea to play hard to get once in a while. Don't just drop everything for them all the time because a woman might start taking you for granted.

. . .

THINK about whether you want to be in a relationship, take your time rather than rushing into it. When you rush into this decision, it will make you look needy and that will lead to be in the friend zone.

20

PLACE TO MEET AND CONVERSE WITH WOMEN SUCCESSFULLY

M any people find it difficult to meet women. However, there are multiple platforms that can help you connect with your soulmate. If you are finding it difficult to meet women, then read on.

Use Online Socializing Resources

Moving from traditional to online dating is one of the biggest gifts we have in this century. It is an efficient, super easy and not too stigmatized platform. Sites such as eHarmony or OKCupid are known for their top quality advanced algorithms that assist the matching process. It takes factors such as lifestyles choices, morals and values for rapid success rate.

INITIALLY, you must be able to pick out a site that fits your precise criteria. Whichever site you select, ensure that you pay consideration to significant factors. For example, if a site does not have a lot of restrictions or questions; then it means you will have a wider pool but not all will be quality. Search for a dating website that necessitates a decent amount of entry barriers to certify that women who interact will be serious.

OBVIOUSLY THE NEXT step is to invest your time in crafting a quality profile. There is no shortcut. Most of these sites will ask a lot of questions which you SHOULD answer so that matches that come as a result are highly compatible.

MOREOVER, another reason that you are yet not successful in online dating is because you talk more than showing organically. So, for instance, you can add photos from various trips if you want to come off as a traveler or someone who enjoys discovering. Women are skillfully proficient at sensing incongruence. So you must let your actions and preferences speak for you.

Attend Parties

Even though we are extremely lucky to have access to several interesting sites and dating apps where we can find singles, however, it is imperative to break free from time to time and explore the world outside the dating bubble. Why? Because we all need to find opportunities to interact with people in our natural habitat. Not everyone desire that their meeting story begins by "we swiped right."

REMEMBER that majority of the women favor that they meet men physically rather than online. They believe that it develops a more natural connection. A real life first meeting permits you to get a feel for a potential partner's personality, their ability to communicate and their sense of humor.

. . .

ONE OF THE easiest ways to meet people is at parties. However, people mostly show up in groups or couples when they show up at a party. This can make it a challenge for men to approach a woman effectively. It is especially true when the woman is tucked in a small corner.

PARTIES IS a platform is filled with golden opportunities. Just know the right techniques and finding a date at a party won't be difficult. As a precaution you must always have your outgoing friends with you so if all else fails, the night just won't be a total waste.

Join Clubs

Not everyone is into the party scene. Some might even love an intimate group to hang around with. In the traditional manner, you can look for local communities that you join. Just like numerous other steps, it is essential to figure out what interests you the most. Not only will you be able to meet new people, but this will guarantee at least one similarity that you both are passionate about.

FOR INSTANCE, if you enjoy reading then joining a nearby book club can do wonders. Similarly, if you enjoy cooking as a hobby, then joining a class can definitely get a girl on your arms. Women love a man who can prepare a decent meal.

MOREOVER, you can easily find any group or a small community for absolutely anything. It is especially true with the introduction of social media. Joining a club will facilitate you to engage with like-minded individuals who will possibly introduce you to people from their circles. You never know when you might get lucky.

ALSO, if you are publicly shy, it might be more comfy to meet your date through a mutual friend or search for a date online. Therefore, networking with compatible individuals, both in real life and online, might be the key for you to locate the one true soul mate in life.

CONCLUSION

Finding the love of your life or someone who complements you is challenging for everyone. This is especially true for men because they function in a different way than women in general. Approaching a woman and then conserving with her appropriately seems to be one of the biggest issues.

This book is all about powerful insights for men who are looking to date and having a meaningful conversation with women without freezing or going blank. It starts off by explaining the differences in the way men and women communicate. Understanding this is imperative because it will allow you to act accordingly and facilitate you to decode a woman's mindset.

Moreover, you will find details about why men fail to attract women and who amongst the crowd gets heard. Humor, emotional intelligence and listening tends to play a vital role when it comes to conversing with a woman.

Likewise, the way you approach also leaves a huge impact. It helps in developing the first impression, which is why you must approach a woman from an angle that they can see you. Approaching from the back can startle them and make them feel threatened.

Planning to talk to a woman is also essential as it will help calm the nerves. You will feel more prepared and confident as you walk up to the woman of your dreams. It is also essential so that you can impress her enough to initiate and enjoy a conversation. Presenting yourself is likely the most important step when conversing with a woman. First impressions last and these impressions help women make a decision even before talking to a man.

Once you have approached a woman, the next step is to make small talk and break the ice. Asking meaningful questions and avoiding distractions are also significant to effective communication.

How to Talk to Women is a comprehensive guidebook that will aid men to attract their soulmate. A chunk of communication is non-verbal which is why the book stresses upon reading and understanding these cues.

Connecting on a deeper level with a woman will help you build lifelong connection. The book offers helpful tips that can assist in building valuable relationships. A reason for failure to attract the woman of your dreams is the anxiety and fear of conversation. This book will help you cope up with this fear so that you are not left alone.

Dating online is a newly emerging arena to meet women. Creating a profile and knowing hacks to have meaningful conversation via texting and chat boxes is essential. You will find valuable information that can help you meet women online.

CPSIA information can be obtained
at www.ICGtesting.com
Printed in the USA
BVHW050017030123
655397BV00029B/1606